CONVERGENCE

Heaven's Destiny Becoming Your Reality

CONVERGENCE

Heaven's Destiny Becoming Your Reality

PATRICIA BOOTSMA

Scripture taken from the New King James Version. Copyright © 1982 by Thomas Nelson, Inc. Used by permission. All rights reserved.

Published by XP Publishing
A department of Christian Services Association
P.O. Box 1017
Maricopa, Arizona 85139
www.XPPublishing.com

ISBN-13: 978-1-936101-43-6

Patricia Bootsma may be contacted through Catch the Fire Toronto:
http://www.ctftoronto.com

For Worldwide distribution

ENDORSEMENTS

Patricia, a spiritual daughter of ours for over 25 years, lives the values that exploded out of the Revival in Toronto, and carries them zealously to multitudes around the world. This powerful book is her life; digging deep into God's Word and soaring high into His Presence, to see healing, miracles, revelation and prayer. *Convergence: Heaven's Destiny Becoming Your Reality* will catapult you into living your Prophetic Destiny! If you're trying to remain lukewarm, don't read this book.

JOHN AND CAROL ARNOTT
CATCH THE FIRE, TORONTO

Patricia is the real deal. She walks in extraordinary integrity and radical love. I believe she is a true prophet of the Lord. I am thrilled to be able to recommend her book, *Convergence: Heaven's Destiny Becoming Your Reality,* and pray that it stirs a greater hunger for intimacy in all those who read it.

HEIDI BAKER, PHD
FOUNDING DIRECTOR,
IRIS MINISTRIES

Patricia Bootsma is one of the most solid, anointed, prophetic mentors I know. In addition to being a respected prophetic leader in the Body, she teaches and nurtures individuals in the prophetic. She has also been used to bring the "prophetic water-level" up in regions and nations. Her book, *Convergence: Heaven's Destiny Becoming Your Reality,* is a must read for any hungry student of the prophetic. It is one of those books that you will probably want to buy two of—one for your own library and another to lend to others. *Convergence: Heaven's Destiny Becoming Your Reality,* with its solid, foundational teachings can also be used in Bible studies and training classes as a lesson topic guide. I highly recommend this book!

PATRICIA KING

FOUNDER, XPMEDIA

Patricia Bootsma is someone I admire deeply. For years she has prophesied with great accuracy and integrity. In her typical fashion, Patricia has written a book that flows from her heart and her life. It is a manual for anyone who wonders how one's current reality can ever catch up to God's prophetic destiny. No matter what your circumstances, you will be blessed and challenged by Patricia's story, as she demonstrates from her own life how one can be mother, pastor, prophet, and international speaker: just listen to His voice and believe!

STACEY CAMPBELL

FOUNDER - CANADIAN PROPHETIC COUNCIL

INTERNATIONAL CONFERENCE SPEAKER AND AUTHOR

Not one wasted word in this rich book! It is pure essence: carefully distilled explanations and practical Godly principles. Read it quickly and you will yearn for a fresh intimacy with God;

digest it carefully and you will dust off your prophetic words and decree God's truth; embrace it fully and you will walk into a new prophetic lifestyle. Thank you, Patricia, for a powerful, succinct pathway to destiny.

CHESTER AND BETSY KYLSTRA
FOUNDERS
RESTORING THE FOUNDATIONS INTERNATIONAL
HENDERSONVILLE, NORTH CAROLINA

DEDICATION

I dedicate this book to my Heavenly Father—You have loved me to life; to Jesus—I'm continually fascinated by Your beauty and to Holy Spirit—how I love Your Presence.

I also dedicate this to John—my earthly bridegroom of over two decades—what a precious gift God gave me in you. And to our six children—Judah, Gabrielle, Aquila, Phoebe, Zoe, Glory Anna and daughter-in-law Bethany.

There is no mother on the planet more proud of her children. The character, gifting and passion for the Lord you continually demonstrate cause me to say, "Surely I am the most blessed among women."

TABLE OF CONTENTS

INTRODUCTION

God cares about prophecy. By His design, 40% of the Scriptures are prophetic messages or stories of revelatory encounters. There are 300 Old Testament references alone to the Messiah and Jesus fits every one of them. 1 Corinthians 14:1 encourages us to desire spiritual gifts, especially to prophesy. Our Lord places a high value on the operation of this gift in our lives and desires for us to walk in the fulfillment of the words He gives us.

Many biblical prophecies will be fulfilled automatically just because God said so—such as Jesus' Second Coming. However, words spoken over individuals, cities, and nations are conditional—their fulfillment is based upon our response. Like the Israelites, we have a free will to choose to enter the Promised Land—or go our own way.

Paul exhorted believers to "wage war" for personal prophecies. How does one wage war for a prophetic word and journey from promise to fulfillment? That question burned in my heart as I sought the Lord about how to walk in the things He promised me through prophecies.

In this book, you will walk beside me on my journey of discovery so the Lord can reveal to you the keys to unlock the doors of your destiny. My prayer is that you will experience convergence of heaven's desire for your life both here on earth and in the glorious eternal realm to come.

"… Thus says the Lord God: 'None of My words will be postponed any more, but the word which I speak will be done,' says the Lord God" (Ezekiel 12:28).

PATRICIA BOOTSMA

1

IT ALL BEGINS WITH INTIMACY

"Set me as a seal upon your heart,
as a seal upon your arm... "
(Song of Solomon 8:6).

CHAPTER 1

Growing in intimacy with Jesus was not on my mind the day my husband came home from his bank job to announce that he had been promoted and we were relocating. We were moving, with our newborn son, Judah, to a sleepy little town two hours north of the city where we lived. Actually, I could see nothing positive in this promotion beyond a small upgrade in the rat race of life. Spiritually, it seemed like we were moving to the desert because we would be leaving a support system of mature believers who were our dear friends.

John and I had met years before at John and Carol Arnott's thriving church in Stratford, Ontario. Even though we lived in London, Ontario, where we both had graduated from the University, we gladly made the one-hour trip to church. My husband had taken Bible courses in preparation for the day he would become a pastor, but at this time, our livelihood came exclusively from his job as an assistant bank manager. I had recently given up my career as a Registered Nurse to become a full-time mother and we led a growing house fellowship, which I had started as a student.

When I heard of John's promotion, I hoped it was not a spiritual demotion and that God had not forgotten the prophecies He spoke over John and me. Even before we knew one another, we had received similar words about working for the Lord in ministry, pastoring, and traveling the nations speaking for Him with miracles, signs, and wonders following our ministry.

Two months later, as I followed the moving truck transporting our meager belongings to a small rented house in a town boasting two traffic lights and one McDonalds, I thought about those prophecies. They seemed like distant dreams, farther away now than ever. Instead of moving closer to their realization, we seemed to be on our way to insignificance, or ...

Another thought intruded on my gloomy musing ... could God be up to something not evident to me? Did He have something up His proverbial sleeve? I began to feel the stirring of excitement and hope as I recalled Solomon's cryptic statement in Proverbs 25:2, "It is the glory of God to conceal a matter, but the glory of kings is to search out a matter." The recollection of that Scripture marked the beginning of my search for intimacy with God.

MY LONELY QUEST

My first lesson began as I sought to find God without the external support of fellow believers to which I had become accustomed. I needed to learn to access intimacy with the Lord by myself—not through another person, ministry, or church.

I had known the way of salvation since I was twelve and had experienced the fullness of the baptism in the Spirit since nineteen. Yet, here I was in a spiritual desert, a 25-year-old wife and mother who hungered for a vibrant relationship with Jesus.

Jesus announced in John 7:37, "… If anyone thirsts, let him come to Me and drink."

David said:

"One thing I have desired of the Lord, that will I seek: That I may dwell in the house of the Lord all the days of my life, to behold the beauty of the Lord and to inquire in His temple" (Psalm 27:4).

As a prophetic picture of the Bride of Christ, the Shulamite woman said to her beloved, "Let him kiss me with the kisses of his mouth—For your love is better than wine" (Song of Solomon 1:2).

Drinking of Jesus … gazing on His beauty … kissing the bridegroom? It was like a foreign language to me! For some reason a fear of intimacy was keeping me from connecting to the heart of God. I knew the Great Commandment was to love the Lord with all my heart, soul, mind and strength (Matthew 22:37). I had heard the Lord beckon me out of merely a dining room relationship with Him into the inner chambers. The outer courts I was familiar with, but that place "beyond the veil," I wondered, what did it look like?

Day after day in our little home in Listowel, I sought the Lord in prayer, through His Word, and by learning to discern the voice of the Spirit. Living miles from everyone and everything familiar, there were no distractions. After John went off to work and once little Judah's needs were tended to, I would pick up my Bible and my journal with a heart determined to find the God of intimacy for which I hungered.

A KEY TO ONENESS

Walking in intimacy or finding oneness with Jesus has to do with a key found in 1 John 4:19, "We love Him because He first loved us." Really recognizing His love for us initiates our love for Him.

> *While gazing on those eyes of blazing fire ... spending time with Him in quiet reflection on His love ... meditating on His words of love from the Bible and from hearing His voice ... my heart was beginning to awaken!*

While gazing on those eyes of blazing fire ... spending time with Jesus in quiet reflection on His love ... meditating on His words of love from the Bible and from hearing His voice ... my heart was beginning to awaken!

Similar to achieving oneness in a marriage, intimacy with Jesus has to be developed. It does not come automatically with the conversion experience just as a marriage is far more than merely saying, "I do" during a ceremony. Time, commitment, and choosing oneness and intimacy are necessary to build and keep the fire of passion burning in our hearts.

Many start out with zeal in their newfound faith or after encounters with realms of Glory. However, discovering the romance of intimacy with Christ requires a determination to pursue God daily, in spite of the monotony of everyday life.

The Languages of LOVE

The popular book, *The Five Love Languages* by Gary Chapman, can help us understand the ways that God shows us His Love. Our Lord speaks all five languages divinely because He *is* love. Yet, love is more than a language; it is a person—the person of the Father, the person of Jesus, the person of the Holy Spirit—three Who are totally united in one Being. God spares no expense in demonstrating His love for us.

He loves us in "words" of encouragement.

Scripture is filled with references to God's love for us and His desire to bless us. The written or logos Word of God, when read and meditated upon regularly, causes truth to penetrate our minds and hearts.

Hearing the rhema word, the still small voice of God, helps awaken our hearts to love. "… My heart leaped up when He spoke… " (Song of Solomon 5:6). When the Spirit whispers, "I love you; you delight Me," receive it as truth and do not ignore or dismiss His repeated attempts to communicate love. Consider how incredible it is that the God of the universe adores you so much that He regularly attempts to communicate His love to you.

The Lord shows His love in "quality time."

He literally has all the time in the world for us. God is never too busy with "more important matters" than to remember us. His eyes are ever on us, and He longs for us to take time to spend with Him.

Seth Yates, a singer and musician at the International House of Prayer in Kansas City, had a dream which he sang in the Prayer Room. He described how the Lord had set a banquet table laden with food and called him to come and dine. In his dream, Seth recalled thinking that he felt that he did not have the time to spend with Jesus because he had so much to do. As his worries overwhelmed him, Jesus merely smiled at him and said, "Sit at my table." That dream became the message of Seth's song to the Bride of Christ. It contains the words, "Where are you going? What are you doing? You were made to sit at His table."

Adam and Eve were hiding in shame after eating the forbidden fruit when the Lord came to walk and talk with them in the cool of the day. Satan had lured them into sin to separate them from intimacy with God. Our enemy will stop at nothing to keep us from spending time in intimacy with the Lord. You may be unaware of it, but there is a war for your intimacy. It can have many forms—busyness, shame, jobs, relationships, quest for the world's goods, and walls of fear set around our hearts to guard us from anything we think may be harmful.

Time is one of our most precious commodities and how we spend it reflects our priorities. Taking some of our time to cultivate intimacy with Jesus is an investment for eternity because our relationship with Him will have no end. Although we will not be married to our spouses in heaven, a far greater relationship with Christ awaits us; one we will have for time without end. Today is your time of Divine Romance; do not allow anything to steal moments of intimacy with the Lover Who cares so deeply for you.

The Lord loves us with His "touch."

Feeling God's Presence and His arms of love wrapped around you is an experience available to every believer. Many have never known the feeling of God's presence and have dismissed it as mere sensationalism. However, Scripture shows us the depth of God's feelings in Song of Solomon 4:9: "You have ravished my heart, My sister, My spouse. You have ravished my heart with one look of your eyes, with one link of your necklace." The Bride in turn expresses in Song of Solomon 5:8: "... If you find my beloved ... tell him I am lovesick!" These strong words express a relationship of passionate, intimate love between Jesus who is the Bridegroom, and we who are the beloved, His Bride.

Ian McCormack, a native New Zealander, was scuba diving off the coast of the island of Mauritius when stung by a deadly Box Jellyfish. As he was dying, he tells of reaching out to Jesus and saying the only prayer he knew, the one his mother had prayed over him, the Lord's Prayer. Finally reaching a hospital, he was pronounced dead and placed in the morgue. Ian remembers spending frightening moments in hell before being brought into the Presence of the Lord. The Lord explained that He had been allowed to see hell to know what He deserved but had escaped.

Before this experience, God had been nothing but a swear word to Ian. He never read the Bible nor attended church. However, in the Presence of the Lord, Ian got a glimpse of eternity with Christ and wanted to remain there. Then he thought of his mother and knew that when she learned of his death, she would be distressed, believing he had gone to hell. Ian was given the opportunity to return to earth and he is now a pastor who proclaims the reality of heaven and hell. While in the Presence of God and after returning to earth, Ian felt waves of love touch his body while he was being healed. He describes it as "liquid love." Ian weeps every time he tells his story of transformation because of God's undeserved love and rescue from eternal damnation.

During the outpouring of the Spirit that began in Toronto in 1994 and continues to this day, millions of people have recounted being touched by God in dramatic ways. Jolts of electricity, waves of warmth, healing fire—the descriptions of God's touch are innumerable and have often been accompanied by a deep change and lasting fruit in the individuals. The most stoic pastors have rolled in laughter on the carpet. Those with hardened hearts have wept when exposed to the power of our Heavenly Father's love.

One of the best ways to cultivate your feeling of the touch of God is to regularly spend time soaking in His Presence. For the past decade, the first thing I do every morning is listen to anointed worship music. This simple act of focusing my attention on the Lord the first thing everyday has radically changed my life. My heart is softened as I feel God's Presence, while I am being filled with His Spirit.

I remember when, as a nurse, I hooked patients up to intravenous drips to give them the liquids or medicine they desperately needed. When I put my ear buds in to listen to worship music, it is as if I am hooking up to a divine IV. I become infused with strength and the fruit of the Spirit: love, joy, peace, patience, kindness, goodness, gentleness, faithfulness, and self-control.

The Bible portrays spending time with God as "waiting on the Lord" and uses eagles to symbolize overcoming believers. When we moved to a new home built for our family in Stratford, Ontario in 2003, I marveled at the address, 40 *Eagle* Drive. Then we engraved in the foundation of our home the words of Isaiah 40:31:

> "But those who wait on the Lord shall renew their strength; they shall mount up with wings like *eagles*, they shall run and not be weary, they shall walk and not faint."

God shows His love with "gifts."

Just imagine, He did not even spare His own Son to give us the gift of intimacy through the shed blood of Jesus. The Father's extravagant giving is reflected in a multitude of ways: He gives the Gifts of the Spirit; He gives financial blessing; He gives authority and anointing. He has even given us the Kingdom: "Do not fear, little flock, for it is your Father's good pleasure to give you the kingdom" (Luke 12:32).

Intimacy is cultivated as we receive the gifts the Father has freely given, and as we give back by walking in His purposes. The greatest gift we can give to God is, of course, our hearts. Aligning our hearts with the Lordship of Jesus and allowing nothing to become more important than Him, is our way of giving back to the One who held nothing back for us.

The Barometer of Our Priorities

Our financial giving is an indicator of the priorities of our heart. I was nineteen when the Lord taught me the value of the tithe. As a student of nursing, I had no income and on one occasion, I had only $10 left in the world. I decided to give it in the offering at church that Sunday. By the end of that week, I had received $100 unexpectedly, which was a lot of money to me at that time. Since then, I have given the tithe (the first 10%) of all financial increase in my life to the Lord, and offerings on top of that, and financial miracles have become the norm.

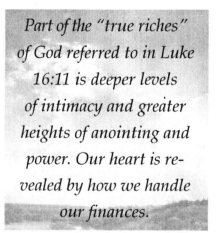

Part of the "true riches" of God referred to in Luke 16:11 is deeper levels of intimacy and greater heights of anointing and power. Our heart is revealed by how we handle our finances.

Luke 16:11 says, "Therefore if you have not been faithful in the unrighteous mammon, who will commit to your trust the true riches?" I believe that part of the "true riches" of God referred to in this Scripture is deeper levels of intimacy and greater heights of anointing and power. Our heart is revealed by how we handle our finances.

God demonstrates His love by His "actions."

How often has the Lord intervened to protect, guide, and open doors of opportunity for us? His love is evident by what He does for us.

Numerous times, I have seen the work of angels in our family. When my daughter Gabrielle was three years old, I heard a terrible crash from her bedroom. I ran to her room and found that a large clothes dresser had fallen to the floor. Gabrielle, however, was seated on the top bunk bed with a sheepish look on her face. She had tried to climb the dresser to get something from the top when it started to topple over. It was a miracle that she was not crushed under the heavy dresser. She later told me that somehow, when the dresser began to fall, she had been picked up and placed safely on the top bunk. That same week, sadly, a three-year old girl in our city died from doing the same thing. While climbing a dresser, it crashed on top of her. I grieved for that unknown child and was grateful for the angelic protection for my daughter.

When our son Judah was seventeen, he was swimming with his father in the waters of the Great Lake located 45 minutes from our home. Judah recalls becoming aware of an undertow and signaled to his Dad that they should turn back to shore. Only hours later, another 17-year old boy who lived minutes from our home drowned in those same waters. I am convinced that the

Lord protects our loved ones from the assignments of darkness because the Word says, "The angel of the Lord encamps all around those who fear Him, and delivers them" (Psalm 34:7).

A Lesson for Living Out a Life of Intimacy

One essential for walking in intimacy with the Lord is to simply hear and obey: "If you love Me, keep My commandments" (John 14:15).

St. Augustine said, "Love, then do what you please." When our hearts are awakened in love, we do not want to displease the One we hold dear. We not only want to keep the commandments in God's Word, we also want to obey the "still small voice" when it nudges us to give financially, speak a word of edification, or give a message of hope to someone in need.

YOUR LOVE SONG

Misty Edwards expresses the heart of God clearly in the song that says, "How far will you let me go? How abandoned will you let me be?" When we truly enter into the journey to intimacy, the question is never "How much can I get away with?" but "How much of myself can I give away?" When we become immersed in His love, we long to be a conduit to give it away: "As I have loved you …also love one another" (John 13:34).

We can only give love and intimacy if we have received it. We cannot give to others that which we do not possess. Living out the Great Commandment to love the Lord our God with all our heart, soul, and mind is only possible after we have learned to receive the love He has for us. When we have experienced how much He loves us, we can become lovers of God.

In the little town of Listowel, this truth became clear to me. Removed from everything and everyone that I held dear, (outside my immediate family) I learned to find intimacy with Him in the deepest recesses of my being. The Holy Spirit within beckoned me to awaken to His call for intimacy and He is lovingly calling you, too.

ACTION STEPS

Listen to the whisper of the Holy Spirit calling you into the Oneness of intimacy as you make these simple steps part of your daily life:

1. Seek the Lord in prayer asking Him to remove any barriers to intimacy and awaken your heart to encounters with His love.

2. Schedule a regular time daily to soak in the Presence of the Lord. Listen to anointed music and reach out for a connection with the Holy Spirit. (My favorite soaking CD is Ruth Fazal's instrumental "Songs from the River.")

3. Set your heart to obey the Lord above all else going on in your life. Let David's cry of Psalm 27:4 be yours, "One thing I have desired of the Lord, that will I seek: That I may dwell in the house of the Lord all the days of my life, to behold the beauty of the Lord, and to inquire in His temple."

HEARING GOD'S VOICE

"...a still small voice"
(1 Kings 19:12).

CHAPTER 2

The book flew across the room hitting the wall with a thud and fell to the floor. "Ahhhh," I muttered in frustration—I had gotten it wrong again. "Words" that I thought were from God turned out to be from a different source since they failed to materialize. The flying object was the journal I used to write out my prayers and the words I believed God had been communicating to me through His still small voice.

I have had a strong desire to hear the Lord since I was a small child. The ordinary croaking of frogs from a pond outside my bedroom window occasionally seemed to articulate, "I love you, I love you." Was I hearing things or was the Lord speaking to me? While riding my pony, I found Him in the wind, blowing through the grass, and in the open expanse of country fields that I grew up exploring.

As a teenager, I longed to hear the voice of God more clearly. Somehow, even then, I knew this was part of my heritage and birthright as a believer. There was never a time in my life when I did not believe I could hear the voice of God; I just wanted more clarity. Certain passages of Scripture would challenge me, such as, John 10:27, "My sheep hear My voice, and I know them, and they follow Me."

My hunger to hear God has led me on an exciting journey through which I discovered a very communicative God.

Technically speaking, Father God is in heaven and Jesus is seated at His right hand. The third part of the Trinity, the Holy Spirit, is with us here on earth, abiding within every true believer. He is our comforter, counselor, teacher, guide, leader, source of power, anointing, giver of gifts, and the One who makes us fruitful.

Another role of the Holy Spirit is to speak to us. Jesus, said in John 16:12-15:

> "I still have many things to say to you, but you cannot bear them now. However, when He, the Spirit of truth, has come, He will guide you into all truth; for He will not speak on His own authority, but whatever He hears He will speak; and He will tell you things to come. He will glorify Me, for He will take of what is Mine and declare it to you. All things that the Father has are Mine. Therefore, I said that He will take of Mine and declare it to you."

The Holy Spirit consistently represents the Father and Son to us. When we seek to "hear" from the supernatural realm, we do not listen outwardly, with our ears, but inwardly with our spirits. The Hebrew word for prophet is Naba, meaning to "bubble up." Prophetic words bubble up into our consciousness from the Spirit who lives in our innermost being.

HEARING AIDS

When I discovered the teachings of Mark Virkler, they changed my life dramatically (see www.CWGMinistries.org). I devoured his book, *Communion With God*, and his teaching tapes like a starving child.

This former Baptist minister explains in his book what happened when he took a year off and devoted it to learning how to hear the voice of God. That time of prayer, reflection, and study brought him to four simple keys found in Habakkuk 2:1-2:

> "I will stand my watch and set myself on the rampart, and watch to see what He will say to me, and what I will answer when I am corrected. Then the Lord answered me and said: 'Write the vision' ..."

Key #1—God's voice in your heart often sounds like a flow of spontaneous thoughts. While we may expect God to speak to us in an audible voice or booming inner channel, more often He speaks in spontaneous thoughts, visions, feelings, and impressions.

Key #2—Become still within so you can sense God's flow of thoughts and emotions. "I will stand my watch (on my guard post)..." Dialing down the busyness of our minds and simplifying our lives helps us tune into the sweet stillness of the Spirit's presence.

Key #3—As you pray, fix the eyes of your heart upon Jesus. "I will...watch to see what He will say to me..." Turning our inner attention to the Lord opens the eyes of our heart and awakens our understanding of the divine flow within. Ephesians 1:18 speaks of the "eyes of our understanding (heart) being enlightened."

Key #4—Journaling, the writing out of your prayers and God's answers, brings great freedom in hearing His voice. Habakkuk 2:2 "Then the Lord answered me and said, 'Write (record) the vision...'" Recording our thoughts at these times helps us tap into a flow of spontaneous words and visions from God. Journaling also makes it possible to test the words we received at a later time to ensure that they align with Scripture and with the character and nature of God.

Judging the Words We Hear

After I threw my journal across the room, the Lord gently urged me to go pick it up. My hunger to hear His voice overcame my fear of making mistakes. Later, I was further encouraged to continue my quest by John Arnott's wise statement, "We need to trust the Lord's ability to lead us more than the enemy's ability to deceive us." I was asking my Father for something that I knew He wanted me to have. He urged me to be patient with myself as I learned to grow in my experience of hearing Him. Similar to a child learning to walk, we will fall down many times, but we must get back up and try again if we are to one day run with confidence. I needed to go through more growth steps and refusing the temptation to quit was the next thing I needed to learn.

Scripture teaches us to judge the prophetic (1 Thessalonians 5:20-21). Whatever is of the Lord will pass His tests and be consistent with the logos Word of God, the Bible. In addition, accurate prophecy will be in alignment with God's nature of love because God is love (1 John 4:8). Because prophecy comes through the Holy Spirit, we know that His words will always be gracious and saturated with the Fruit of the Spirit: love, joy, peace, patience, kindness, goodness, faithfulness, gentleness, and self-control (Galatians 5:22-23). Consequently, anything we hear that makes us nervous, anxious, or lacking in peace we can judge as not from the Spirit of God. All true words from the Lord will also be consistent with the "Testimony of Jesus," which is everything recorded that He said and did both on the earth and in heaven. "The testimony of Jesus is the spirit of prophecy" (Revelation 19:10).

The Father's words are always edifying in some way, exhorting, and comforting as the Bible declares in 1 Corinthians 14:3. Even when we are corrected or confronted to come up higher in our character and deeds, it will be embedded in hope and encouragement.

Before meeting the man who became my husband, I spent three and a half years dating a guy that I thought I would marry. He had found the Lord through my witness. During journaling, I thought I heard God say that this man was the right one for me. However, no one who could hear God's voice and those in authority over me, including my pastors and parents, believed that he was the right one. Although confirmations did not come, I stubbornly clung to my beliefs, ignoring this important key for judging prophetic words. If spiritually mature, trusted people do not confirm the words we believe we have received from the Lord, alarm bells should go off warning us not to proceed (1 Corinthians 14:29).

Idols Create Confusion

We build idols in our heart when we hold things, desires, or people in overly high esteem and mistake the voice of our idols for God's voice. When we want something intensely, we may believe that we hear God say we can have it. Yet, all the while, our strong will is shouting louder than God is as He voices His true intentions for us.

After suffering much unnecessary pain, I finally surrendered this relationship to the Lord, and asked Him to sit on the throne of my heart and I surrendered my will to His. That same night I dreamed that this man had another girlfriend while maintaining his relationship with me. That morning, I called a mutual friend and asked outright if my dream was true. She confirmed it and I finally had the courage to end this tumultuous relationship. Later I wondered, why had I not heeded those warnings three and a half years earlier? This was a hard lesson to learn but a very valuable one: God will always confirm what is of Him, particularly when it is an important decision. He will never leave us in blind confusion.

PERSONAL PROPHECY—THE RHEMA WORD

When Satan tempted Jesus, He replied with authority, "It is written, 'Man shall not live by bread alone, but by every word that proceeds from the mouth of God'" (Matthew 4:4). In this passage, the Greek expression translated "word" is "rhema," which means "the spoken, uttered word of God."

Hearing God's voice, I believe, is a part of the "daily bread" Jesus told us in the Lord's Prayer to expect from God. It is the regular partaking of food for our spirit. Just as proper nutrition sustains our physical bodies and is necessary for growth and health, hearing the voice of our Lord is required for our spiritual health and growth.

Not partaking of this spiritual sustenance (rhema) when it is established in the logos word of God can make us susceptible to spiritual diseases—religious spirits, an ineffectual spiritual existence, or, worse yet, a lukewarm, intellectual-based relationship with the Lord. Just as we need to sit down to eat food everyday and make the effort to prepare, chew, swallow, and digest a meal, we also need to take the time to listen, position ourselves to hear the voice of the Lord, as a daily part of our spiritual diet.

"...Your thoughts toward us cannot be recounted to You in order; if I would declare and speak of them, they are more than can be numbered" (Psalm 40:5).

"How precious also are Your thoughts to me, O God! How great is the sum of them! If I should count them, they would be more in number than the sand" (Psalm 139:17-18).

God's thoughts toward us are more numerous than the grains of sand on the seashore. That is astounding! Many times, I have walked a beach and thought of this passage. Imagine how much sand is in a desert. One handful of sand is said to contain approximately 10,000 grains and yet, God's thoughts toward you outnumber the sand. When

> *Imagine how much sand is in a desert. One handful of sand is said to contain approximately 10,000 grains and yet, God's thoughts toward you outnumber the sand.*

you hear His voice, you are simply tapping into that stream of thoughts. There is never a shortage of His thoughts toward you. You never have to convince God to speak; He is an extremely talkative Father. Jeremiah 29:11-13 explains the nature of His thoughts toward us:

"For I know the thoughts that I think toward you, says the Lord, thoughts of peace and not of evil, to give you a future and a hope. Then you will call upon Me and go and pray to Me, and I will listen to you. And you will seek Me and find Me, when you search for Me with all your heart."

However, there are other voices fighting for attention in the continuous inner dialogue going on within our soul and spirit. When we give our attention to this inner communication we can hear negative thoughts about ourselves, other people, how we have been unjustly treated, and it goes on and on. When I first began to pay attention to what was swirling through my mind, I was distressed by what I found. "Putting on the mind of Christ" was not going to be as simple as I once thought. I needed to war daily against a mental bombardment by the soulish, carnal nature and from demonically inspired whispers that echoed hopelessness, defeat, and reminders of where I did not measure up.

"Casting down arguments and every high thing that exalts itself against the knowledge of God, bringing every thought into captivity to the obedience of Christ" (2 Corinthians 10:5).

This is not a quick fix but it is an effective one. I had to surrender years of negative thought patterns to the Father by an act of my will. Replacing negative thoughts can be as simple as purposely interchanging them with positive ones but overcoming them requires God's help and His grace.

Remember, "The weapons of our warfare are not carnal but mighty in God for pulling down strongholds" (2 Corinthians 10:4). The strongholds of our mind come down by the power of the Lord in partnership with our willingness and desire for change. The mind is indeed a battlefield and what better way to win that battle than to focus on the numerous thoughts of our Heavenly Father consistently coming to us, thoughts full of life, victory, and love.

As I began positioning myself to hear the voice of God, the "words" that came to me were often challenging to my beliefs about myself. The Lord would declare how much He loved me; that He had a great destiny for me and with His help, I would walk in the fullness of His calling. Previously, I had low self-esteem; I saw my faults vividly and barely noticed my virtues. Yet, the Father's words of encouragement nudged the potential He had placed in me even when it was difficult for me to believe it could be true. Romans 10: 17 says, "Faith comes by hearing, and hearing by the word of God." Again, the Greek expression translated "word" in this passage is "rhema." When God's Word is spoken into our spirits, it causes faith to arise for what He says to us. His destiny, His plan, and His way often contradict our limited, finite beliefs but if we dwell long enough on His words, we will eventually lift our eyes to see things from a heavenly perspective.

Transformation Is the Outcome of Revelation

Bill Johnson, pastor of Bethel Church in Redding, California, states, "The first reason for revelation is to transform us." Life altering revelation awaits us if we take the time to position ourselves in faith to hear the voice of God. My life has been radically altered by regularly hearing and recording the words of life spoken to me by my loving Heavenly Father.

Recording God's words to us is advantageous in many ways:

- It helps us to remember them.

- It makes it possible to look back and meditate on what God spoke yesterday, last month or years ago.

- It helps us test the accuracy of words.

- It allows us to honor His words and makes them more meaningful to us.

- It helps us grow in the ability to hear Him.

The exercise of journaling helps us to become increasingly more accurate as we develop more disciplined and regularly cultivate intimacy with God to hear the voice of our Beloved.

Journaling Is Simple ... Anyone Can Do It

What I have found most effective is prioritizing journaling each morning, incorporating it in my personal time with the Lord. I start by writing the open-ended question: What do you want to say to me today, Father?

Then I position myself comfortably and quietly to listen with pen and paper in hand and simply write down what I hear. When He has finished, I may ask Him specific questions about that day, about things of concern to me, and other things for which I need my heavenly Father's counsel.

> As I go about my day, the line of communication remains open to dialogue with the Lord as I walk, drive, and move through each moment. I do not write down all those dialogues but I may record pertinent tidbits later. Journaling is not the only way to tap into the flow of God's words. However, I have found that it helps me hear Him at any time and that it causes a flow of the prophetic to bubble up whenever needed.

My husband and I both rely heavily on hearing the voice of God for parenting. We know we have a perfect Father in heaven who understands how to parent better than anyone else does. Regular requests for His wisdom in this area have yielded wonderful results: six children who passionately love the Lord and are growing in His destiny for them.

Listening for the voice of the Lord for insights concerning your workplace, your relationships, and for minor and major decisions will bring supernatural assistance.

After borrowing Peter's boat to use as a platform for an outdoor meeting, Jesus told Peter to launch out into the deep and let down his fishing nets for a catch. This made no sense to Peter who had worked all night but caught nothing. Yet, Peter said, "… At Your word (rhema) I will let down the net" (Luke 5:5). Because of his obedience, Peter brought in a great haul of fish. When we listen and live according to God's rhema words for us, we can also haul in blessing and increase.

Increase and a Mess?

"Where no oxen are, the trough is clean; but much increase comes by the strength of an ox" (Proverbs 14:4). I believe this can be applied to those who would hear God's voice and live a prophetic life. Without the prophetic, the stall is clean, but when it is in your life, there can be a bit of a mess to clean up at times. This Scripture is saying that the very thing that brings "increase" can be messy. You will make mistakes in the process of growing and becoming strong in this gift, everyone does. You also need to "feed" this gift by exercising and utilizing it. However, hearing the voice of God brings the increase we need for every area of life.

ACTION STEPS

1. Take a moment, right now, to position yourself to hear the voice of the One Who loves to communicate with you.

2. Dial down the busyness of your mind ... tune into the spontaneous flow of thoughts that come to you ... fix your attention on Jesus ... and simply ask, "What do you want to say to me?"

3. Write down what you hear, even if it is only a single word or short phrase. Relax and allow the words to flow. His thoughts are constantly streaming toward you, as numerous as the sand—simply receive them.

CHAPTER

3

HEALING OF THE HEART

"The thief does not come except to steal, and to kill, and to destroy. I have come that they may have life, and that they may have it more abundantly"
(John 10:10).

CHAPTER 3

My thoughts drifted again to the question that had puzzled me for years: "Why do I always end up dating men who mistreat me?" It seemed like I had a sign hovering over my head saying, "Attention dysfunctional men—I'm attracted to you." Nice guys—the kind who opened car doors, gave flowers, and sent sweet cards and letters—did not interest me. Why was I attracted to the very men who were not good for me?

Meanwhile, deep in my heart, there was hurt and resentment toward my father. The arguments, inconsistencies, and fits of anger had left a chasm between us filled with unforgiveness and bitterness. I called him by his first name, unwilling to honor him as my father.

However, the "dots" had yet to be connected between my choice in men and my relationship with my natural father.

One day, in utter frustration at yet another failed relationship, I cried out to the Lord, "I'm so sick of dating. I never want to date again. Just tell me the name of the man you want me to marry!" (I didn't know at age 22, what I know now, that God would guide me to His choice in my future spouse and that it was unnecessary for me to date several men, breaking my heart or theirs in the process. We teach our children about courtship and waiting for God's best which will be confirmed in His time.)

I was shocked to hear the near audible voice of the Lord speak into my spirit the name, "John." Thinking I might as well press for more information, I asked, "John who?" Again, I received a reply, "John Bootsma." I had heard there was a fellow who recently moved to my city with that name but I had never met him. I had no idea how old he was or any other personal details. I responded to God, "I can't marry a John, my sister married a John." My reasoning went like this: since my oldest sister had married a man named John, we had our quota of Johns in the family.

A few weeks later, I met John Bootsma at church. He was a banker and seemed friendly and handsome enough. He pursued a relationship with me, and since I thought I heard God say he was going to be my husband, I responded. However, early on I noticed behavior that caused unfavorable feelings to well up inside my unhealed heart. John opened the car door for me, gave gifts, and treated me kindly. My unhealed heart had no place for men who expressed kindness and tenderness. Consequently, I was not attracted to him and pushed him away.

By the mercy of God's timing, Carol Arnott had recently discovered the teachings of John and Paula Sanford on healing of the heart. She had returned from their ministry center excited about her life-transforming experience. I immediately signed up for this ministry, ready—no, desperate—for breakthrough.

FINDING AND FEELING FORGIVENESS

I was aware that the Bible taught forgiveness and I had made feeble attempts to forgive my dad. However, I soon began to see that extending forgiveness was crucial to receiving forgiveness. It became clear that many issues in my life were not about what had been done to me but my wrong reactions to them. The Lord took me on a journey of deep forgiveness toward my father. Layer upon layer of pent-up resentments had to be surrendered to the Cross. Specific situations would come to mind that I needed to forgive. Mentally and emotionally, I ripped up IOUs that I had held so tightly, finally letting them go and freeing debt I had felt was owed to me.

Forgiveness usually begins as simple obedience without the corresponding emotions; however, often feeling forgiveness follows the action. Forgiveness is not optional for believers, regardless whether the person who has wronged us states regret or remains unrepentant. The reward for forgiveness is not vindication but freedom.

Unforgiveness has been compared to wishing for someone's death while you drink poison. Unforgiveness always leads to bitterness and bitterness can defile many (see Hebrews 12:15). Forgiveness of others and at times ourselves is a required step to walking in the fullness of our destiny.

JUDGMENT'S BOOMERANG EFFECT

Next came the Lord requiring me to repent for all my "judgments." Romans 2:1 says:

> "You are inexcusable, O man, whoever you are who judge, for in whatever you judge another you condemn yourself; for you who judge practice the same things."

Sowing judgments causes us to reap in kind. The copious judgments I made toward my father were coming back on me. In the areas where I judged him, I was unknowingly cursing myself to receive the same thing. Judgments handcuff us to the very offenses and wounds that we despise and even cause us to become like those who wounded us. Why do children of alcoholics marry or become alcoholics? Why do those who have been abused become abusers?

The sacrifice of Jesus on the Cross purchased our freedom... Freedom is available for those who understand how to receive it and apply it!

These troubling questions have been the subject of speculation by psychiatry for years. However, by ignoring God's spiritual laws and principles they only find superficial reasons and never make a real breakthrough. The sacrifice of Jesus on the Cross purchased our freedom. Therefore, just as we needed to apply the power of the Cross by faith for our salvation, so the breakthrough of the Cross has to be applied to the wounds and entanglements of our heart. Freedom is available for those who understand how to receive it and apply it!

Sowing and Reaping Works Both Ways

The spiritual law of sowing and reaping applies to both bless-ing and cursing; it operates in the same way for good and evil. Galatians 6:7-8 warns:

> "Do not be deceived, God is not mocked; for whatever a man sows, that he will also reap. For he who sows to his flesh will of the flesh reap corruption, but he who sows to the Spirit will of the Spirit reap everlasting life."

I was doing plenty of "sowing to the flesh" because of the dishonor I held toward my father. Consequently, I was reaping dishonor toward myself through others.

When we judge someone as being controlling, it opens us up to be controlling. If we judge our mother as being uncaring, it makes us vulnerable to becoming similar in our parenting. If we judge our spouse to be stingy, it can contribute to our embracing the very same tendency.

A Simple Principle That Can Save Much Heartache

1. Repent for sowing to our own destruction by the judgments we have made.

2. Pray to break the cycle of negative reaping and be set free.

3. Begin a pattern of positive sowing with our words and actions and reap the blessing.

Honor Reward

The fifth of the Ten Commandments is the only one with a promise attached for those who obey:

> "Honor your father and your mother, as the Lord your God has commanded you, that your days may be long, and that it may be well with you in the land which the Lord your God is giving you"(Deuteronomy 5:16).

God did not add, "Only if your parents are good, loving Christians who never treat you wrong." It simply says to honor them. How to live out honor is a question I asked the Lord many times. When I finally repented of my judgments and dishonor toward my father, I did not instantaneously experience emotions of goodwill and feelings of adoration for him. I attended the family Christmas celebrations, sent him a Father's Day card, and hoped that was good enough. Yet when we moved closer to my parents in 2003, the Lord began to challenge me to show greater levels of honor. Not only does the Lord want us free of the negative effects of past hurts, He wants to restore relationship wherever it is possible.

The Lord began instructing me to show love to my dad in ways that would actually speak to him through his "love language." My mother and father visit a coffee shop each morning, something I never desired nor felt like I had the time to do. Yet, the nudges of the Lord directed me to go and sit in the coffee shop with them to hear their stories of growing up in the war years, talk about what other family members were doing, or relate what was going on in my family. Amazingly, this simple act of obedience, a couple times a week, yielded results far beyond my expectations. My father began to communicate openly with me; my heart warmed to him and he began speaking the words

I had longed to hear, "I'm so proud of you." "I love you." Showing honor requires action, and divinely inspired actions open doors for reciprocation.

GENERATIONAL CURSES, THE GOOD NEWS

While working as a registered nurse, I often saw family patterns of ill health. Likewise, family patterns of divorce, poverty, anger, accidents, or abuse are usually more than mere coincidence. A family pattern of curses is clearly displayed in the famous American Kennedy family line. Death by gunshots, skiing accident, airplane crash, and cancer are but a few examples of what the Kennedy family has endured. One leading magazine showing the picture of the deceased John Kennedy Jr., carried the blatant headline "The Kennedy Curse."

Exodus 20:5-6 states:

> "For I, the Lord your God, am a jealous God, visiting the iniquity of the fathers upon the children to the third and fourth generations of those who hate Me, but showing mercy to thousands, to those who love Me and keep My commandments."

Deuteronomy 7:9 declares:

> "Therefore know that the Lord your God, He is God, the faithful God who keeps covenant and mercy for a thousand generations with those who love Him and keep His commandments."

The good news is the blessings on the lineage of the righteous far outlast those of the sinful. However, the generational inheritance of iniquity must be broken for us and our descendants to walk in freedom. If you don't want freedom for yourself, at least do it for your children.

I mentioned how I found myself gravitating toward unkind men. My dad's father was known as a hard man, and there were stories of his verbal and physical abuse. My dad was one of only four boys among 16 siblings. When my mother and I studied the history of my aunts, we made a disturbing find—11 of my dad's 12 sisters had married unkind men lacking in character. I was on track to continue the family pattern until I received the freedom that came from the Lord.

With the help of the Holy Spirit, generational curses can become known and broken through identification and repentance.

Cultural Curses and Their Bondages

At times, what is needed is freedom from generational traits passed down culturally. Both of my parents were born in The Netherlands. Even though I was born in Canada, the Lord prompted me to investigate my Dutch heritage. I had been struggling with a strange kind of unworthiness as well as a prideful heart. I would oscillate between lack of confidence and thinking I could do it all myself.

I discovered that "The Netherlands" means "the lowlands." When I prayed for the breaking of any low mentality I had inherited, something shifted over my life. I also uncovered a saying in Holland that went like this, "God made the world, but the Dutch made Holland." The axiom came from the Dutch taking land from the sea by putting up dikes. When I repented of and broke this inheritance of independence and pride, a positive change occurred. You may recall that Daniel repented for himself and his ancestors' disobedience in order to break the curse that caused them to live in bondage (see Daniel 9).

With the help of the Holy Spirit, generational curses can become known and broken through identification and repentance.

UNGODLY BELIEFS

Chester and Betsy Kylstra, dear friends who have pioneered a ministry for healing the heart called "Restoring the Foundations," clearly explain the power of "ungodly beliefs." At their core, ungodly beliefs are lies we have believed about others, God, the world, and ourselves. These falsehoods hold us captive to self-destructive traits or behaviors. Consciously or unknowingly, we hold these beliefs through family heritage, personal experiences, cultural ways, or things learned from others. They are like train tracks that direct the way our mind travels, which influences what we expect and receive. For example, my expectations about men were ruled by the belief that, "All men are mean and treat women badly." That was my expectation, so it was what I encountered. Once broken, however, ungodly beliefs no longer have the power to hold us captive to negative expectations.

Freedom Is At Hand When ...

1. We repent of wrong beliefs,

2. break our agreement with them in prayer,

3. invite the Lord to illuminate godly expectations and attitudes,

4. and replace our ungodly beliefs with His truth.

Freedom from ungodly attitudes and expectations changed my outlook on God, others, the world, and myself. My thoughts became scripturally based, true beliefs. This is the renewing of the mind spoken of in Romans 12:2.

DELIVERANCE FROM DEMONIC STRONGHOLDS

Unforgiveness actually opens us up to the demonic or "torturers" (see Jesus' parable in Matthew 18:15-34). Likewise, judgments, dishonor, bitterness, generational curses, ungodly beliefs, and deep hurts can also provide permission for demonic influence or oppression.

Even though Simon the Sorcerer had found salvation (Acts 8:13), he still displayed evil and needed deliverance. Peter said of him, "For I see that you are poisoned by bitterness and bound by iniquity" (Acts 8:23).

Christians can be oppressed by demons and I was one who needed deliverance! After giving forgiveness, repenting, and withdrawing the access I had unknowingly given to demonic powers, deliverance came easily. That is what it means to clean out our spiritual house and to keep it clean by closing doors of permission for demonic entry. This requires healing of the heart and making right choices (Matthew 12:43-45).

When we find ourselves ensnared by self-destructive patterns and behavior, we should address the spirits behind our actions and ask the Lord where they have gained access to our lives.

The power of healing in a completely surrendered heart yields life-changing results. We are transformed when we submit to the Holy Spirit's nudging to deal with the wounds of life. As we embrace the healing of our hearts, we become positioned to soar into our God-given destiny.

I am very happy to report I did marry that wonderful man named John Bootsma and with a healed heart (all the while continuing to surrender to the Lord as He revealed further areas needing surrender and healing) we have thoroughly enjoyed over twenty years of marriage, growing in love for each other each passing day.

ACTION STEPS

Opening our hearts to divine healing starts with a simple prayer like David's cry found in Psalm 139:23-24.

1. Would you pray it with me? "Search me, O God, and know my heart; try me, and know my anxieties; and see if there is any wicked way in me, and lead me in the way everlasting."

2. As we ask the Lord to heal and reveal to us all the areas blocking the fullness of our destiny, He is faithful to do so. Choosing forgiveness again and again is your key. Even when our emotions want to "hang on" to the hurt or injustice, the way of the Father is the way of forgiveness and keeping our hearts pure. Ask the Lord to open your eyes to reveal every person you need to forgive.

Information on the ministry of Chester and Betsy Kylstra, "Restoring the Foundations," is available on the Internet along with powerful testimonies of lives transformed. Go to www. restoringyourlife.org.

CHAPTER

4

THE FATHER'S LOVE

"Behold what manner of love the Father has bestowed on us, that we should be called children of God!"
(1 John 3:1).

CHAPTER 4

Understanding how much our Father in Heaven loves us is crucial to knowing who we are in Him (our identity) and what we are called to do (our destiny).

When we really know we are children of a loving Father who happens to hold the universe in the palm of His hand, it really changes our outlook on life. Similarly, when we actually recognize our identity as His child, we have a desire to get into the destiny for which we were created or as Jesus put it, "… I must be about My Father's business" (Luke 2:49).

IDENTITY IS REVEALED THROUGH RELATIONSHIP

As a child, I could grasp the idea that Jesus was real and loved little children like me. The pictures in my books and on

Sunday School walls lovingly portrayed Him as carrying sheep and holding children. Relating to Jesus in the manger and Jesus on the Cross was believable and attainable.

However, the idea that I have a Father in heaven baffled me and took much longer to grasp. Undoubtedly, the inability to understand God as Heavenly Father was related to my poor relationship with my earthly father while growing up. As I mentioned previously, forgiving my dad and repenting of my judgments was a huge step toward establishing a good relationship with him. However, it also created an enormous change in how I related to my Heavenly Dad. The concept of "father" that we develop in our relationship with our natural fathers carries over to how we feel about our Father God. Hence, it is very import to obtain healing in our relationships with our fathers, whether they are alive or even if they have gone on to eternity. Do it to improve your relationship with Father God.

Love cannot be analyzed; ... it must be experienced.

Experiencing God's love is so important that the enemy of our souls will try his hardest to keep us from perceiving it.

I am convinced we can never reach the end of the revelation of how much our Heavenly Father loves us. As I write, I am overlooking the Atlantic Ocean at Myrtle Beach, South Carolina. Many times the Lord has whispered that His love for me is as "vast as the ocean." While looking out over this great expanse of water, it is clearer now than ever before that His love has no bounds—He is love!

Love cannot be analyzed; it is beyond intellectual comprehension;

it must be experienced. Experiencing God's love is so important that the enemy of our souls will try his hardest to keep us from perceiving it. Within a profound revelation of His love, there is life for the dead areas of our soul. Wounds, walls around our hearts, busyness, and fears are the enemy's weapons to block our perception of God's love.

Embracing Sonship or Daughterhood

Years ago, Jack Frost came to speak at Toronto Airport Christian Fellowship on the Father's love. After his teaching session, I could only remember one thing. In fact, he asked a question that so completely pierced my heart I did not hear another word he spoke. He asked, "At what point did you cease to be a son or a daughter?" This simple question left me dumbfounded. As soon as possible, I found a quiet place where I could get alone with God and asked the Lord why I was so disturbed by that question.

The Lord revealed to me something my mind had forgotten but my spirit had not. At age 14, I had made the decision that I no longer needed a father. The pain of that relationship had left me so disappointed, I decided that I did not need any more fathering and would be better off without it. That was when I began earning money to sustain myself, buying my own toiletries and clothes. I also began saving up to leave home, and leave home I did at age 17. I paid my way through college and university. I bought my own car, even though my dad had purchased cars for my siblings. John and I paid for our own wedding, even though my dad had paid for an extravagant wedding for my older sister.

At 14, an independent spirit had taken hold of me and I decided I would not be a daughter any longer. I thought it had served me well, not being dependent on my dad for anything and becoming a strong-willed and self-sufficient person. However, here I was years later, a grown, married woman with children, still battling insecurities while trying to project to the world the image of a super-confident woman of God.

I felt like an orphan on three levels:

> First, even after a measure of healing in this area, I still found relating to Father God on a deep level to be difficult.

> Secondly, although I had forgiven my natural dad years ago, I still did not want to be with him and rejected his attempts to father me.

> Lastly, I felt a gap between my spiritual father and myself. Although I loved John Arnott dearly, there was an inexplicable chasm between us.

I wept as I repented to the Lord for my spirit of independence and for my vow to no longer be a daughter ... and His love and forgiveness washed over me. However, there was more for me to do. As uncomfortable as it was, I went to my dad and asked him to forgive me for my decision to not be his daughter. He forgave me, and that was another step in the healing of our relationship. John Arnott was out of the country, so I sent him an email explaining the journey I was making toward finding the fatherhood of God. I repented for the areas where I had not embraced being his spiritual daughter. He wrote a beautiful letter back to me, forgiving and blessing me as his spiritual daughter. Something powerful shifted in my life after this season and I was able to walk in my identity as a daughter of God to a much fuller extent.

ENCOUNTERING THE FATHER'S LOVE

The predominant characteristic of the wonderful outpouring of the Spirit that began in Toronto in 1994 was the manifestation of the Father's love received by many. In my time as an Associate Pastor at Toronto Airport Christian Fellowship and since becoming involved in itinerant ministry, it is difficult to estimate the numbers of testimonies I have heard of the life-altering transformation of those who had a supernatural encounter with the Father's love. It often happened while doing "carpet time," slain in the power of the Spirit.

I experienced the Father's love as waves of warmth, liquid love, washing over me, and I still experience it to this day. Regular soaking in the Presence of God each day is necessary to keep our "love tank" full and overflowing.

Once while worshipping at home with my guitar, I was taken up in the spirit to stand before the throne of God. In the natural, I was still in my living room playing my guitar. However, in the spirit, through my inner eye, I could see the Father beckoning me to come nearer to Him. As I approached the throne, He lifted me onto His lap. Then the strangest thing happened. The throne became a rocking chair and He held me tight against His chest while rocking me back and forth. In the natural, I began to weep under the power of this amazing expression of love.

Still playing my guitar, I heard the Father sing a song over me which I began to play on my guitar and sing myself. This love song continued for about 20 minutes, and it was all in perfect rhyme. I knew this had to be real because I am not capable of singing a spontaneous song in perfect rhyme in my own ability. I will always remember that encounter—it changed me forever. I now know beyond a shadow of a doubt, that I am a dearly loved child of my Father in Heaven, whose love for me is as vast as an ocean. God has a personal encounter with His love for everyone who seeks it.

Encounters with the Father's love enable us to live much more confidently; not in ourselves but in His unfailing love and good intentions toward us. This "knowing" enables us to step out, take risks, and trust that He will make "… all things work together for our good …" (Romans 8:28). Even if we make mistakes, our Father's love is sufficient to rescue us.

Robert McGee, in his book titled *The Search for Significance*, created clever equations about self-worth.[1] The ungodly equation is:

Self-Worth = My Performance + Other's Opinions of Me

The sum of this equation is very inconsistent because our performance may vary from situation to situation and the opinions of others can be erratic and fickle.

By contrast, the godly equation for self-worth is:

Self-Worth = His Performance + His Opinion of Me

Because God is stable and forever consistent, our self-worth never varies from His point of view. His performance and His opinion of us does not change due to our behavior. He loves us unconditionally. He loved the world while it was still drowning in sin (John 3:16).

I appreciate what Mike Bickle, the Director of the International House of Prayer in Kansas City states, "I am loved by God, I

[1] Robert McGee, *The Search for Significance*, (Nashville, TN: W Publishing Group-Thomas Nelson Inc.) 1998.

am a lover of God, therefore I am successful." That is the true definition of success.

THE CHARACTER OF FATHER GOD

Encountering the Father's love brings us into contact with the Father's character. Because "God is love" (1 John 4:8), He cannot help being loving; it is Who He is. I have also discovered the Father is:

- Kind (Psalm 117:2)

- Slow to anger (Nehemiah 9:17)

- Trustworthy (Psalm 37:5)

- Merciful (Exodus 34:7)

- Gracious (1 Peter 2:3)

- Generous (James 1:17)

- Dependable (Daniel 3:17)

- And fun (Hebrews 1:9).

What an amazing Daddy we have!

Just as Jesus perfectly reflected the Father, we too are encouraged to look, act, talk, and live like our Father in heaven. We are enabled to do this by fully embracing His character. In other words, when I really grasp how "kind" the Father is to me, it enables me to be kind to others. When we grasp the fact that He is "slow to anger, abounding in mercy," we then can have more patience with others and give them mercy. However, we cannot give what we have not first received.

DESTINY—LOVED TO LIFE

Insecurity is a common characteristic of the "orphan heart." We will be insecure at our core, when we do not know who we are or how much we are loved. We seek to cover up this insecurity with things such as—performance, the way we look, our position or social status, and the pretenses we put on with others. Yet, all the while, there is a battle of insecurity raging within. If our longing to be accepted and valued is not found in the Father's love and satisfied there, we will do whatever it takes to gain approval wherever we can get it.

It has been said that the singer Michael Jackson was searching for the love that seemed to evade him. Apparently, he did not have a good relationship with his father while growing up and felt driven to be the best of the best. The love and acceptance of his fans became his motivator. Yet, when the adoring fans had gone home, he felt empty and turned to medication to make him sleep, wake him up, and to dull the pain of his father's perceived rejection.

The singer Sting was once asked why he worked so hard to produce more and more songs. Even though his father had passed away, he replied that he was driven to write and play songs that would make his dad proud of him.

I lived for years with the orphan heart, even though I had many personal prophecies about the great things I would accomplish through the call of God on my life. However, walking in that destiny requires risk-taking, and the orphan heart constrains us to stay in familiar and safe places to minimize the potential for rejection. In essence, this dysfunctional heart keeps us from crossing the Jordan to the Promised Land for our lives.

Caleb and Joshua were the only two of the twelve spies who explored the Promised Land who were able to enter its goodness. They believed the land could be taken in victory and the others did not. What did Caleb and Joshua possess which the other spies lacked?

Scripture reveals they had a "different spirit" (Numbers 14:24). They knew the Lord delighted in them (Numbers 14:8), and unlike the others, they did not have an orphan heart. They knew that God would come through for them and give them victory (Numbers 13:30). This kind of relationship with God is required to cross our "personal Jordans." Going to a higher level requires us to take risk by faith that is rooted in the Father's love and character. He is faithful; He will not leave us as orphans (John 14:18).

Opening our hearts to our Heavenly Father's massive love, forgiving our earthly fathers where needed, and repenting of not walking in sonship, are all keys to walking in a greater revelation of God as our Father. Living in this revelation empowers us to step out into our God-given destiny with the confidence that Father will be there for us. He would never set us up for failure.

I am so grateful when I board an airplane to speak in yet another country that I can do so with the revelation that my Father is coming with me. He is ever faithful and because I trust His faithfulness, I can walk out my destiny … and you can do the same.

> *A crucial aspect of your destiny is to be a son or daughter to your loving and all-powerful Heavenly Father.*

We need fathering whether we are eight years-old or eighty-eight. No matter what your job is—mother, father, businessman, media person, church leader, teller, politician, clerk, doctor, educator, entertainer, athlete or whatever—a crucial aspect of you destiny is to be a son or daughter to your loving and all-powerful Heavenly Father. He will enable you to soar in your purpose because He loves you to life.

ACTION STEPS

1. Allow the Lord to search your heart regarding things that hold you back from being a son or daughter to Him, to spiritual fathers, or your natural father.

2. What emotions are conjured up when you think of your natural or Heavenly Father? Do you need to repent of rebellion or a decision to not be a son or daughter? Allow the freedom that comes through forgiveness to wash through your heart. Make the decision to forgive. Your feelings must not be allowed to affect this decision; it is non-negotiable. Just as we must receive forgiveness from God for sin, we must also forgive those who have sinned against us (Mark 11:26).

3. Ask the Lord to envelope you in His love and to heal wounds that keep you from this revelation. Declare regularly:

   a. "My Father in heaven loves me."

   b. "I walk in a spirit of sonship."

   c. "I choose to be a child enveloped in my Father's embrace."

CHAPTER

5

LIVING A PROPHETIC LIFESTYLE

*"Pursue love, and desire spiritual gifts, but
especially that you may prophesy"
(1 Corinthians 14:1).*

CHAPTER 5

L iving a prophetic life is not reserved for a select few prophets. That may have been the case in the former Old Testament covenant. Prophets such as Moses, Isaiah, Nathan, Ezekiel, Jeremiah, Joel, and Amos spoke on behalf of God to the people of Israel. However, when Jesus died on the Cross for the sins of the world, an amazing thing happened. The veil in the temple was ripped in two from top to bottom; God Himself removed the barrier to accessing His presence into the Holy of Holies. This new newfound access to the Glory Realm and the subsequent outpouring of the Holy Spirit at Pentecost made it possible for all believers to function prophetically and encouraged them to do so. If you desire spiritual gifts, you can have them the same simple way you access salvation—through faith.

Salvation is available to everyone; however, to receive it one must repent of sin and confess Jesus as Lord. Through faith we enter this door and by faith we receive the infilling of the Holy Spirit, empowering us to be witnesses (Acts 1:8). Likewise, it is through faith we operate in the Spiritual Gifts (1 Corinthians 12). These gifts become available to every Christian when the Holy Spirit enters their life.

CLAIM THE PROPHETIC

1 Corinthians 14:1 says, "Desire spiritual gifts, but especially that you may prophesy." Notice the word "desire" is used to describe how we are to crave spiritual gifts, especially prophecy. The Greek word for desire is *zeloo* and it means "to be zealous for, to burn with desire, to pursue ardently, and to desire eagerly or intensely." We are divinely instructed to passionately go after the prophetic. 1 Corinthians 14:31 actually states that we "can all prophesy." Living prophetically is available to all who desire and passionately pursue it by faith.

> *1 Corinthians 14:1 says, "... Desire spiritual gifts, but especially that you may prophesy." Living prophetically is available to all who desire and passionately pursue it by faith.*

We are instructed to pursue this gift from heaven but it also is something in which we have to grow. A beautifully wrapped present may be given to you but if you fail to open and actually partake of the gift, it is only a meaningless pretty box. Many believers have stared at the prophetic giftings of a few individuals in wonder but never considered that they, too, have received this gift. There are those called to the office of a Prophet (Ephesians 4:11), one of the five-fold ministry gifts of Christ to the Church to equip the saints for the work of the ministry. The ministry gifts given to a few, however, should not be confused with the Gifts of the Spirit that have been given to all believers.

The body builder with big, bulging muscles was not born with more muscles than you or I have. We all have the same number of muscles! It is not a question of whether you have them but how you use them. Similarly, we each have the same promise to operate in the gifts but, like the body builder, the frequency of its use will determine its growth in your life. Paul stated those "by reason of use have their senses exercised" (Hebrews 5:14).

JOURNEY INTO THE PROPHETIC

First, you must believe the Lord wants you operating in this precious gift. I frequently encounter people who have the ungodly idea that the prophetic is not for them. (This belief is contrary to Scripture.) They say things like, "I'm not prophetic; I'm more logical." "I can't hear the voice of God." "I never have dreams or get visions." That kind of thinking will keep you from functioning in your gifts. If you have had those thoughts or stated that you are not suited for the prophetic, you will need to repent to unblock the channels God would use to bring the revelatory into your life.

You may have noticed that 1 Corinthians 14:1 does not say there is a certain type person who should or should not pursue spiritual gifts. Rather, God encourages all to desire them.

Some who have risked operating in a spiritual gift have had a bad experience. They may have been silenced by another or made an embarrassing mistake. The natural tendency when this happens is to back away, consciously or unconsciously, from your gift. You may need to forgive someone or even yourself to get back on track. If one has witnessed or been told of abuses of the prophetic or if they have been taught this gift is not for today, forgiveness may need to be extended to the immature or false prophetic person or the one who spoke against prophetic gifts.

When my husband was a child, his family was lured into a religious cult. John's parents thought they were following God's leading when they became involved with a man who professed to be a last-days prophet. He convinced John's parents to sell their property, give the money to the group he led, and move onto property he owned. It soon became apparent to them that this sect was in no way biblical or bearing good fruit. Unfortunately, the damage to the family was substantial, both financially and emotionally. Because John's father had thought he was following God's voice by joining this charlatan, the experience left John with a need for healing regarding the authentic prophetic. Understandably, he never wanted to be misled as his family had been.

John is very knowledgeable of the Scriptures and logical in his thinking. This led him to believe that he was not "wired" prophetically. I call him a walking concordance because I can ask him about any passage of Scripture, and he will tell me the book and verse where it is found.

John's journey into the prophetic required an uncovering of layers of negative experiences with what had been called "prophetic," and a rejection of lies he had come to believe that were contrary to God's Word.

I recall decision-making conversations we had early in our marriage that always seemed to come to the same end. I gave my opinion based on what I believed the Lord was saying. John explained his opinion based on the facts. Usually our opinions did not align and he would say, "That doesn't make sense." I would respond, "You are just speaking out of reason. We need to have faith." Of course, wisdom and understanding along with faith and prophetic insight make a winning combination and our 20-year marriage has proved just that, providing us many opportunities to learn from each other.

John forgave the cult leader, forgave his father, and repented of judgments he made concerning prophetic gifts. Additionally, John repented of believing the lie that he was not prophetic and asked the Lord to open up this gift in him ... and the transformation has been amazing. John hears God's voice regularly and prophesies with accuracy and authority.

Once the barriers to receiving revelation are removed, it is a good time to ask for divine inspiration to flow (Matthew 7:7-11). We have a loving Heavenly Father who wants you to prophesy. Therefore, when you ask in faith, you will receive.

PRACTICING THE PROPHETIC

As mentioned in Chapter Two, the practice of journaling to hear God's voice is a wonderful way to exercise the prophetic gift of spiritual hearing. I have exercised this gift nearly every day for more than two decades and I can tell you from personal experience, the gift grows with use.

Soaking in the Presence of the Lord, particularly on a regular basis, sensitizes us to the Holy Spirit and sharpens our ability to receive revelation. Cultivating intimacy by just being in the Lord's presence during soaking opens our heart to hear Him.

A good knowledge of the Scriptures is important to keep us grounded in truth, because all prophetic revelation must be tested through the lens of God's Word. We also receive prophetic revelation through the Word. In fact, the most important way to hear God is through Scripture.

Another key to exercising the prophetic gift is simply to invite the Lord to speak to you throughout the day using any means He chooses. In the room where I am writing this chapter, there are electro-magnetic waves all around me that are invisible to the eye. I know they are present because my laptop is picking up the waves that enable my internet connection. There are also radio waves used by cell phones in this room because my cell phone shows a strong signal. There are likely TV waves here as well although I do not have a television. The point is—with the right receiver antenna, you can capture those invisible communication waves. Likewise, believers are wired with a prophetic receiver, and if we learn to put up our "spiritual antenna," we will pick up heavenly communications.

Remember from Chapter Two that the thoughts the Lord thinks toward us are as numerous as the grains of sand. Hence, in prophesying over individuals, we are merely picking up on what He is thinking toward them. Those thoughts are numerous because He always has many great things to say about His children.

FACETS OF THE PROPHETIC

There are three main aspects to the prophetic:

1. Revelation—what you receive from the Lord

2. Interpretation—what it means

3. Application—what you do with it

We have already discussed a few of the ways to receive divine communication. Let us consider more of the more common ways God speaks to us. (This is not meant to be a comprehensive list.)

1. God's Word—Scripture is the most important way we hear God speak. Paul encouraged Timothy with these words:

"The Holy Scriptures, which are able to make you wise for salvation through faith which is in Christ Jesus. All Scripture is given by inspiration for God, and is profitable for doctrine, for reproof, for correction, for instruction in righteousness, that the man of God may be complete, thoroughly equipped for every good work" (2 Timothy 3:15-17).

2. Still small voice—When God interacted with Elijah at a critical time, His voice was not in the wind, earthquake, or fire but in a "still small voice" (1 Kings 19:11-12). Often God's voice can sound like our own thoughts. When He chooses to communicate subtly, His thoughts invade ours (Psalm 40:5).

3. Visions and Pictures—Paul's prayer of Ephesians 1 includes a petition for the eyes of our understanding (or heart) to be enlightened. Why is this important? Paul answers the question in Ephesians 1:18-19:

"That you may know what is the hope of His calling, what are the riches of the glory of His inheritance in the saints, and what is the exceeding greatness of His power toward us who believe, according to the working of His mighty power."

In other words, having our inner eye enlightened is important to knowing our calling. Jesus said of Himself:

"Most assuredly, I say to you, the Son can do nothing of Himself, but what He sees the Father do; for whatever He does, the Son also does in like manner" (John 5:19).

We may have visions or see prophetic pictures as we ask and position ourselves to receive them or they may simply come as we are going through life. Yet, the inner eye or inner communication with the Father should be ongoing and can be developed. Like Jesus, we too can learn to discern what the Father wants to do through us each day.

4. Dreams—Although not all dreams will be from God, this is an important method the Lord uses to speak to His people. Our tendency to dream "heavenly" dreams will increase when we honor our dreams. This includes:

a. Writing them out

b. Praying into them

c. Paying attention to our dreams

d. Dialoguing with God about them

e. Obeying instruction given in them

The Lord appeared to Solomon in a dream to ask him what he desired (1 Kings 3:5) and in a dream an angel appeared to Joseph and told him to take Mary as his wife (Matthew 1:20). Dreams were used to tell Joseph and Mary to flee to Egypt (Matthew 2:13); to come back to Israel once the danger had passed (Matthew 2:19-20); and to relocate in the region of Galilee (Matthew 2:22).

I have often experienced warnings in dreams so that I can intercede against evil plans and invite the Kingdom of God to invade in a specific situation. Hence, if you receive negative dreams, pray about them but do not immediately assume what you saw will happen—your prayers will make a difference!

5. Word of Knowledge—A word of knowledge is simply insight or information given divinely to a person who would not otherwise know it (1 Corinthians 12:8). This gift is particularly helpful in prophetic evangelism where words of knowledge about an individual often helps open their hearts to the revelation of a God who knows all things about them and loves them (1 Cor. 14:24-25).

6. Word of Wisdom—When the Lord gives divine instruction, blueprints, or insight, it is a word of wisdom (1 Corinthians 12:8). As we ask for wisdom in life circumstances, God has promised to give it liberally (James 1:9).

7. Discernment—Sometimes referred to as "impressions," discernment is the ability to differentiate what is of God from that which is not (1 Corinthians 12:10). When evil masquerades as light, discernment is required to distinguish between things that are pleasing to God and those that are not.

My discernment about which movies are acceptable for my children to watch and those that are not, has grown over the years. A "check in my spirit" indicates unacceptable movies. I can often discern their suitability from just hearing the title or seeing the ad. We need to pay attention to our impressions (sometimes called gut instinct).

As we become more given to the Lord, more sanctified, our impressions and discernment will increase in accuracy.

8. Peace or Lack of Peace—Since peace is a fruit of the Holy Spirit (Galatians 5:20), the Spirit uses peace as a means for communicating whether something is right or wrong. Particularly when we make decisions, we need to ask ourselves if we have peace about the path we have chosen. John and I have found there is safety in ensuring that we both have peace before proceeding with an important decision that affects our family. If one or the other lacks peace, we will not go forward. This practice has repeatedly saved us from problems and mistakes.

9. Circumstances—Doors that open and doors that close can be indications of God's will. If we bang on a door that simply refuses to budge, it is not always the devil holding it closed. It may not be God's best for you or the timing may not be right. When the disciples came to a city that refused them, they were instructed to shake the dust off their feet and go elsewhere (Matthew 10:14). When Paul found himself shipwrecked on the island of Malta, in the natural it was a disaster; however, it opened an opportunity to bring the gospel of salvation and healing to that land (Acts 28).

10. Things in the Natural that Convey a Supernatural Message—Nature itself speaks of God and His handiwork (Psalm 19:1). How can one deny the existence of God when you see the multitudes of stars, the complexity of the human anatomy or the beauty of a sunset? Additionally, the Lord can use seemingly ordinary things to speak to us—a newspaper heading, a billboard, even an object that crosses our path at a specific moment in time.

Once, John and I were traveling a country road while talking about the children's ministry at our church. We recognized they needed help and we were discussing the possibility of taking turns leading the ministry and other options. At that moment, we came upon a car with the license plate ACTZ 636. Immediately we said to one another, "Acts 6:3-6, I wonder what that says." I got my Bible, found the reference, and read how the apostles handled a similar situation in their ministry to widows and orphans. They decided to seek out others to lead this department. They commented, "… We will give ourselves continually to prayer and the ministry of the word" (Acts 6:4). Scripture then goes on to describe how they chose Stephen and six others and commissioned them for this ministry. Amazingly, within a couple months of this incident the Lord sent us a man named Stephen (Stephen, what a coincidence!) to lead our Children's Ministry.

11. Other People—The Lord certainly uses others to speak to us. They may be giving a prophecy (1 Corinthians 14), or simply speaking to us casually when something they say resonates as a word from the Lord. Preachers and teachers certainly communicate to us from the Lord but so do little children sometimes. When our daughter Zoe was six years-old, she scribbled a note to my husband, "Dad I want you to come home." That note struck him powerfully and he knew it was also a word from the Lord that he had allowed himself to become too busy and he needed to spend more time at home with the family.

12. Angels—Biblical precedence for angelic activity is found throughout the Bible.

God uses His angels to ...

a. Deliver messages (Daniel 9:21-22)

b. War with the demonic (Daniel 10:13)

c. Protect (Psalm 91:11-12)

d. Bring freedom (Acts 5:19)

e. Minister to God's people (Hebrews 1:14)

f. Worship the Lord and do His bidding (Psalm 103:20-21)

When I was eight years-old, two individuals came to my family's farm and spoke to me. They told me of things to come in my life, many of which have already been fulfilled. They also spoke of a great harvest of souls I would see during my lifetime. I have never forgotten that event because it "branded me" for the rest of my life with a desire to know and serve the Lord. When I asked my mother, who was working nearby, about the people who spoke with me, she replied, "What people?" Later, I was to read in Hebrews 13:2 that angels can appear in human form.

13. Audible Voice of God—The Lord spoke audibly on numerous occasions in the Bible. One of the most significant times was at Jesus' baptism when the Father affirmed His Son by saying, "You are My beloved Son; in You I am well-pleased" (Luke 3:22).

My grandmother was in great pain with arthritis for years. One day while on her knees praying for others, she heard the audible voice of God boom out, "Pray for yourself." Stunned and accustomed to only praying for others, the message had to be repeated three times before she complied and was instantly healed of arthritis for the rest of her life.

INTERPRETING THE PROPHETIC

When the butler and baker of the Pharaoh were placed in prison with Joseph, they were troubled by dreams they could not interpret. Joseph said to them, "... Do not interpretations belong to God ...?" (Genesis 40:8). Also, when King Nebuchadnezzar demanded that his wise men not only tell him the interpretation but also the details of his dream, Daniel replied:

"... The secret which the king has demanded, the wise men, the astrologers, the magicians, and the soothsayers cannot declare to the king. But there is a God in heaven who reveals secrets, and He has made known to King Nebuchadnezzar what will be in the latter days" (Daniel 2:27-28).

Interpretation of dreams, visions, and prophetic revelation comes from God. If we leave Him out and reduce it to merely the accepted meaning of certain symbols, we have done nothing more than psychics can do.

Certain objects, symbols, or people remind us of related themes which, gives them a special meaning to us that others may not have. A dog to one may mean a friend, but in another's dream may invoke fear or dislike. In other words, there is some truth to symbols holding certain meanings in prophetic revelation but to interpret the prophetic solely based on the recognized meanings of symbols is not the best because it removes our personal symbolism and God from the explanation.

The Lord will reveal the meaning of our revelation. The more we grow in Him, the more clear revelation becomes. I have also noticed in the many years I have spent training prophetic people that the more you grow in the Lord, the more you have literal dreams. Additionally, if you are a participant in your dream, it is more likely that the dream is meant for you. If you are merely an observer in your dream, it may hold a broader interpretation.

There are pitfalls to interpretation, such as having an idol in our heart. If we greatly desire something, we may "hear" God saying we are going to get it when actually our will is imposing a skewed interpretation. Additionally, the following can all lead to a faulty interpretation: unhealed wounds of the heart, unforgiveness, willfulness, ongoing sin in one's life, or a lack of revelation of the Father's love.

APPLYING THE PROPHETIC

Living a prophetic life may cause us to receive revelation from heaven never meant to be shared on earth. I once heard a prophetic man say, "Prophets are known on earth for what they say but they are known in heaven for what they don't say."

Amos 3:7 says, "Surely the Lord God does nothing unless He reveals His secret to His servants the prophets." Often the Lord wants to reveal His secrets to us merely because we are intimate with Him. Sometimes He shares them for us to proclaim, other times for us to pray into, and at other times merely because He wants to share with His intimate ones.

Marc Dupont said, "Prophecy is the spring board into the pool of prayer." I remember receiving words about the prophetic gift on my life and being excited, yet also receiving words about being an intercessor and not being particularly impressed. My idea of an intercessor was a depressed person in a back room praying against evil. That sounded boring to me and I preferred the excitement of being a prophetic voice.

The Lord began to teach me how the prophetic call and the call to intercession are linked hand in hand. He also showed me the fun and even the privilege it was to be a person of prayer, and that He rewarded those who sought Him in prayer (Isaiah 62:11). There is an exciting life to be found in prayer. We sometimes forget that the prophets of the Bible were also intercessors!

WARNING: Negative revelation—forewarnings of tragedy or insights into what the enemy is plotting—must first be bathed in prayer and receive a clear go-ahead from the Lord before being shared.

Those who constantly receive negative revelation often have a pattern of belief that emphasize how big the enemy is rather than how much bigger God is.

I have been both a prophetic voice in churches as well as a pastor (and still am) and I can say from firsthand experience that pastors usually do not want to hear dark, warning revelation. In fact, that kind of prophetic word has alienated some pastors from the prophetic and from intercessory types. We need a clear belief in how big God is and how effective our prayers are in thwarting the plans of darkness. To quote John Arnott, "Big God, itty, bitty devil."

Practically speaking, application of prophetic words in the body of believers should involve submission of that word to whoever is in charge of the meeting prior to giving it. It may be a pastor or the meeting's host who needs to hear what the Lord is showing you before it is shared publicly. I will not give a prophetic word unless asked when attending a service where the leadership does not know me. Rarely would my husband and I release someone to share prophetically in our church that we do not know and trust.

The character of the person is important in determining the relevance and reliability of the word. Should someone stand up from the back of an auditorium and shout out a word, it is dishonoring to those whom God has put in leadership. Additionally, there are appropriate times to share prophetic words. If one has battled in knowing if their word is from the Lord, and finally decides it is but the speaker has started his sermon, the timing for the word has simply passed. Words can be written out and given to leadership, to be judged and viewed later.

Prophecy bathed in love is a precious tool able to bring many into a closer fellowship with their Creator.

1 Corinthians 13: 2 states:

"And though I have the gift of prophecy, and understand all mysteries and all knowledge, and though I have all faith, so that I could remove mountains, but have not love, I am nothing."

The application of prophecy requires a person to be one who

"lives to love." Prophecy without a love for the Lord or for His Bride can be a dangerous, destructive weapon. Prophetic insight into the sins of individuals called out publicly has led to humiliation, fear, and loathing of the gift. Prophecy bathed in love is a precious tool able to bring many into a closer fellowship with their Creator. However, if one does not love the Bride of Christ, they should not pursue prophecy.

In Chapter Two, I shared the tests for judging if a revelation is actually from the Lord and they certainly apply here as well:

1. Does it align with Scripture (2 Timothy 3:16)?

2. Is it consistent with the loving nature of God (1 John 4:8)?

3. Are the fruit of the Spirit present (Galatians 5:22-23)?

4. Is it in some way edifying, exhorting, and comforting (1 Corinthians 14:3)?

5. Is the word consistent with the testimony of Jesus (Revelation 19:10)?

The words of God will stand the test of time and they are revealed as truth when they take us deeper in relationship with Him and further into our destiny.

ACTION STEPS

Pursue the gift of prophecy by asking the Lord to awaken it in your life.

1. Position yourself regularly to hear the voice of God.

2. Ask for dreams and visions.

3. Honor revelations you receive by writing them down in a journal, praying into them, and obeying directives from the Lord confirmed by seasoned prophetic people.

4. Practice prophesying as opportunities arise in small groups with other believers, as well as on the streets with those who need to know the love of God (1 Corinthians 14:24-25).

CHAPTER

6

PROPHETIC DECREES

*"You will also declare a thing, and it will be
established for you; so light will shine on
your ways"*
(Job 22:28).

CHAPTER 6

L ord, what about the prophecies?" It was more of a whiny complaint than a question. "All those words You have spoken over us about pastoring, going to the nations, and being used by You to extend your kingdom—why are they not being fulfilled?" I knelt on the floor in our tiny home in Listowel and wept as I poured out my heart to the Lord. John was at his job as the Assistant Branch Manager of the Royal Bank of Canada. Three-year-old Judah and 20-month-old Gabrielle were playing nearby with their toys.

Since the time I was eight years old, I knew there was a calling on my life to go into the world to tell people about Jesus. As I shared in Chapter Five, I had a visitation from angels in human form who spoke words of destiny; words that caused my little heart to burn to know and obey God. After that encounter, I had recurring visions of being on a stage with others looking out over a sea of dark faces, people who were coming to Jesus, and there were miracles, signs, and wonders in abundance. I knew that it was a vision of a great harvest.

John too had dreams of being mightily used of the Lord in ministry both inside and outside of the church. It seemed like every meeting we attended where a prophetic person was speaking, we were picked out of the crowd to be given prophecies regarding God's call on our lives to minister as pastors and to help extend the kingdom of God.

Yet, none of that was happening or even beginning to happen; instead John was working at a bank and I was a stay-at-home mom. Mind you, John seemed to pastor many in his bank as people shared with him their deepest problems and the tellers confided struggles in their marriages. The District Bank Manager, a man with no children whose life was wrapped up in his job, could not understand the kind, caring side of John and often implored him to spend more time on things that would produce profits for the bank and spend less time listening to "bleeding hearts" as he called them.

As a mom, I loved my children deeply and enjoyed the daily discoveries motherhood brought. I knew that being a wife and mother was a higher calling than going to the nations or being a spiritual leader in a church. Yet, I could not forget the prophecies I had received through others and directly from the Lord. The beckoning to follow my call was unrelenting. A holy restlessness consumed my soul. Although I had given up my nursing career and any hopes of being used in medical missions when I gladly embraced the role of motherhood, I sensed a rebirth of the dreams of ministry that I had laid down. I asked myself, "Was it possible to be a mother and a minister, too? Could I have both?"

My dreams would not die … the Voice beckoning me onward continued.

DON'T COMPLAIN, PROCLAIM

John's patient, persevering character shone through as he faithfully went each day to his job at the bank. I knew inside he was dissatisfied with the pressures of the financial world and longed to be caring for souls, full time; however, he never complained.

Mine was another story as I frequently poured out my dissatisfaction, disillusionment, and complaints to the Lord. Was there some sort of secret, I wondered, for getting my prophecies fulfilled? I felt that I actually did not need another prophecy. What I needed was a manifestation of the prophecies I already had in bountiful supply.

Then the voice of the Lord rang clearly in my spirit, "What are you doing about the prophecies?" "I'm complaining about them," I replied in honesty. "Start calling forth your prophecies," He patiently answered, "Believe them … decree them!"

Like a drink of cold water on a hot, thirsty summer's day, revelation poured into my spirit. THE PROPHECIES OVER MY LIFE WERE CONDITIONAL UPON MY RESPONSE! Likewise, prophecies over a family, a church, a city, or a region are all conditional upon corporate, collective responses. I saw something I had never seen before—the missing piece to the fulfillment of God's call upon my life. I no longer had to sit idly by, merely hoping and waiting for them to happen, I had a role to play in the fulfillment of God's words over my life!

TWO ESSENTIAL STEPS FOR PROPHETIC FULFILLMENT

First, you must have faith in the clear, confirmed word of the Lord. Mary the mother of Jesus modeled this kind of faith and the Bible says of her, "Blessed is she who believed, for there will be a fulfillment of those things which were told her from the Lord" (Luke 1:45).

We enter the door of fulfilled prophecy initially by believing what the Lord said is true, even when circumstances argue the opposite. Alignment of our mind, heart, and belief system with the words from the Lord creates a womb in which those dreams are nurtured for their birthing.

Additionally, our words (which emanate from our hearts and belief system) are either powerful catalysts or deterrents to prophecies being fulfilled. When the Lord spoke to my spirit to decree my prophecies, I did not realize the power of declaration until I witnessed its results. I immediately began marching around our home speaking forth His prophecies over us:

"I call forth the pastor in my husband."

"I call forth the ministry anointing in the church you have ordained for us."

"I decree we have a calling to impact nations for your Glory."

Regularly, I recited back to the Lord the things He already knew because they were His words over John and me. I grabbed hold of them as truth and refused to let go. I very much wanted the destiny He was offering.

Six months later, my husband had a dream. It was similar to the dream Paul had of the man from Macedonia beckoning him to come minister there (Acts 16:9). In my husband's dream, John Arnott was beckoning him to come and help him at his church.

94

Toronto Airport Christian Fellowship, pastored by John and Carol Arnott, had been experiencing renewal for a year at this time. We first encountered this wonderful outpouring on January 31, 1994. After receiving prayer, I began spinning like a top, around and around, before landing on the floor under the power of the Spirit. It was like the unraveling of a mummy's bindings. Afterward I felt so free. Also, a passionate love for the Lord was awakening in my heart. Like a liquid, His love flowed into my being. We returned to Toronto to attend these life-altering meetings as often as we could go.

> *We enter the door of fulfilled prophecy initially by believing what the Lord said is true, even when circumstances argue the opposite.*

After John's dream, we contacted John and Carol to find out if we could help them with the work in Toronto. The response was divinely orchestrated; they warmly invited us to join their team. They were overwhelmed with the day-to-day operations of the revival the Lord had given them and desperately needed help.

On May 23, 1995, we entered employment at Toronto Airport Christian Fellowship on their leadership team; later we became part of the Pastoral team. The Lord had answered my decrees! I saw first-hand how to get prophetic words off the shelf and into reality by partnering with the Lord through declarations.

THE PROPHETIC PARADIGM

The Jews were taken into captivity in Babylon in 586 B.C. Sixty years later, the Lord put it on the heart of a king of Persia, Cyrus, to permit and to assist the Jews in returning to Jerusalem and rebuilding the temple of the Lord. Returning to their broken land and restoring the temple was a daunting task. Ezra 5:1,2 states:

> "Then the prophet Haggai and Zechariah the son of Iddo, prophets, prophesied to the Jews who were in Judah and Jerusalem, in the name of the God of Israel, who was over them. So Zerrubbabel … rose up and began to build the house of God which is in Jerusalem; and the prophets of God were with them, helping them."

> "So the elders of the Jews built and they prospered through the prophesying of Haggai the prophet and Zechariah the son of Iddo. And they built and finished it, according to the commandment of the God of Israel" (Ezra 6:14).

Notice the encouragement and the determination that arose as they heard the word of the Lord and walked in it.

Prophecy is intended to encourage you to build a life pleasing to the Lord, to prosper, and to fulfill your destiny.

We find the conditional aspects of prophecy or destiny in many passages of Scripture. The life of Solomon is an example. The Lord actually appeared to Solomon twice. The first time was in a dream when He asked Solomon what he wanted (1 Kings 3:5). Solomon replied that he desired an understanding (literally a "hearing") heart to judge or lead the people. The Lord was pleased with his request and gave Solomon not only great wisdom beyond his request, but also immense riches and majestic honor.

The second visitation is recorded in 1 Kings 9. It was after Solomon dedicated the temple to the Lord. At this time, the Lord spelled out the price for establishing Solomon's lineage on the throne of Israel forever;

"Now if you walk before Me as your father David walked, in integrity of heart and in uprightness, to do according to all that I have commanded you, and if you keep My statutes and My judgments, then I will establish the throne of your kingdom over Israel forever, as I promised David your father, saying, 'You shall not fail to have a man on the throne of Israel.' But if you or your sons at all turn from following Me, and do not keep My commandments and My statutes which I have set before you, but go and serve other gods and worship them, then I will cut off Israel from the land which I have given them; and this house which I have consecrated for My name I will cast out of My sight" (1 Kings 9:4-7).

Sadly, even though the Lord appeared twice to Solomon, giving him wisdom and blessings, Solomon took 1000 wives and concubines, which he "clung to in love" (1 Kings 11:2). Many of them were foreign wives and they turned his heart away from the Lord. The Lord became angry with Solomon and this was the beginning of the end for the Davidic dynasty.

John Arnott often warns of three common areas of weakness that can bring downfall to a leader: girls, gold, and glory. As with Solomon, the fulfillment of personal and most corporate prophecies is conditional upon our response.

The Weight of Our Words

Proverbs 18:21 states, "Death and life are in the power of the tongue, and those who love it will eat its fruit." When we fully grasp how important our words are in determining the course of our lives, we learn to use them more carefully. Like pebbles thrown into a pond, the ripple effect of our words can be far reaching.

> "But I say to you that for every idle word men may speak, they will give account of it in the day of judgment. For by your words you will be justified and by your words you will be condemned"(Matthew 12:36-37).

James 3 makes clear the power of the tongue by comparing it to the rudder of a ship or a bit in a horse's mouth. It is such a small organ but it is oh so powerful! You may recall from biology class that the tongue has the highest concentration of muscle mass of any body part. Although it is small in size, it is powerful in that it has a powerful impact for good or bad.

The Lord shared with me early in my marriage that I had the capacity to build John up or tear him down—by the things I said to him and about him. This insight put a measure of the fear of the Lord in me and I determined that I wanted to be a life-giving wife. I understood that my words needed to reflect that decision.

A three-part answer for how to overcome evil is provided in Revelation 12:11: "And they overcame him by the blood of the Lamb and by the word of their testimony, and they did not love their lives to the death."

In addition to what has been accomplished in our behalf by Jesus on the Cross and our wholehearted abandonment to God, this passage makes it clear that our testimony is part of the formula for living as an overcomer. Testimony means "witness, historical attestation, or evidence." What testimony are we speaking about others and ourselves? Our words influence those around us to walk in greater victory or defeat. Constant belittling or pointing out faults causes discouragement, which weakens the spirit and only makes matters worse.

Words not only affect the hearer but also the one who speaks them. Jesus said that it is not what goes into the mouth that defiles but what comes out (Matthew 15:11). James also speaks of the ability of the tongue to defile our whole being (James 3:6). When feeling discouraged or down, pay attention to what you are speaking. The cause and effect of our words is real. We actually discourage ourselves when we speak negatively.

James also associates the person who learns not to stumble in their words with becoming perfect or mature. The Greek word teleios means "spiritually mature" and able to bridle or control the whole body (James 3:2). If we cannot control our tongues, it is much more difficult to control selfish desires ... unhealthy sexual impulses ... and addictions. We must take the power of our words very seriously; they can make the difference between life and death.

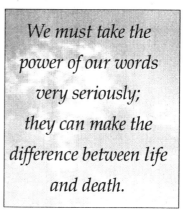

We must take the power of our words very seriously; they can make the difference between life and death.

PROPHETIC DECREES

A simple definition for prophetic decrees is "speaking in agreement with God." We do this by purposing to fill our minds and mouths with the truth of God's Word, both Scripture (logos) and the rhema words spoken to us prophetically.

Joshua 1:8 describes the path to prosperity and success:

"This Book of the Law shall not depart from your mouth but you shall meditate in it day and night, that you may observe to do according to all that is written in it. For then you will make your way prosperous, and then you will have good success."

The Hebrew word translated "meditate" in the preceding Scripture is *hagah*, meaning "to reflect, to ponder aloud to oneself." In Hebrew tradition, to meditate upon the Scriptures is to repeat them quietly in a soft, rhythmic way. Regular repetition of key Scriptures and prophetic words creates a womb for birthing those words in our lives and ministries.

How did God create the world? He spoke and the emptiness shone with light, and that which was without form and void became substance at His Word. Similarly, when we begin to declare with faith the words of God, things shift, circumstances change, and obstacles come into alignment with His will. We are to "call those things which do not exist as though they did" (Romans 4:17) and to speak to the mountain (which is any obstacle) to be removed (Matthew 17:20).

The Apostle Paul exhorted Timothy to wage war for the prophecies given over his life (1 Timothy 1:8) "... to stir up the gift of God in himself" (2 Timothy 1:6) ... and to "not neglect the gift of God within him given by prophecy" (1 Timothy 4:14). Paul knew the importance of faith-filled actions and words as part of walking in fulfilled prophecy.

Bill Johnson puts it this way, "Nothing happens in the kingdom unless there is first a declaration."

Children and Decrees

The children's saying, "Sticks and stones may break my bones but words will never hurt me" is utterly false. Words can have enormous power over children, affecting not only their future but also their present sense of security and well-being.

Years ago, I began to create declarations to speak daily over my children and it has born great fruit. Decrees like:

"My children are passionate lovers of God."

"My children will only marry the person the Lord has for them."

I pray the Prayer of Jabez (1 Chronicles. 4:10) over each of them daily, inserting their names. For example:

"Oh that you would bless (Phoebe) indeed and enlarge (Phoebe's) territory, that your hand would be with (Phoebe) and that you would keep (Phoebe) from evil, that (Phoebe) may not cause pain."

Every day John and I speak over our children phrases such as: "You are the head and not the tail, you are above, and not beneath, you will lend to many nations and never have to borrow. You are smart and understand your schoolwork. You have favor with God, and people. You are a Bootsma—you are set apart for righteousness."

The effect of these words of life spoken over our children has been significant. They have lived up to the life-giving proclamations and they are walking in ever-increasing expressions of their God-given destinies.

Directions For Designing Decrees

1. **Regularly (daily is best) declare words of life** over yourself, your family members and loved ones, over your church, city, and nation; then watch as it bears

fruit. Here are some helpful tips for creating and using powerful decrees:

2. **Be Consistent:** Persistence in decrees is needed. When our youngest child, Glory Anna, was born with a protrusion in her mouth, we were told it was a ranula (which is a problem with the salivary gland) and that it could only be repaired surgically, but the surgery could be delayed for a few years. We began to decree healing over our precious child, who we did not want to go through surgery. Four years later, the ranula suddenly disappeared. A consistent faith walk is necessary.

3. **Be Brief:** When writing decrees, it is best to summarize the point in a sentence or two. This makes the decree easier to use. For example, "I submit to God, draw near to Him, and walk in obedience," summarizes one of the desires of my heart.

4. **Ensure the Decrees are Consistent with Scripture and According to the Nature of God:** This is simply a test to ensure that your declarations are in accordance with the will of God. One of my decrees is "I live in perpetual, intimate communion with the Lord and have peace. His Presence is always with me." This comes from Matthew 28:20 and Philippians 4:7.

ACTION STEPS

Begin today to reshape your world by bringing your faith-filled words into alignment with the heart of God for you and those around you.

1. Write three decrees of things prophesied over you (or given to you by the Lord) that have yet to be fulfilled.

2. Write three decrees that are the opposite of things with which you struggle. (Decrees are never negative but the positive opposite.) For example, if it is financial difficulty, call in breakthrough using Proverbs 10:22 and other Scriptures.

3. Lastly, write three decrees that express godly desires you have (find Scriptures upon which to base your words).

7

LOVE FOR THE WORD

"Your word is a lamp to my feet and a light to my path"
(Psalm 119:105).

CHAPTER 7

Meditating on the written Word of God ignites within us a connection with its Author. Speaking to Jews, Jesus said:

"You search the Scriptures, for in them you think you have eternal life; and these are they which testify of Me. But you are not willing to come to Me that you may have life " (John 5:39-40).

Jesus is saying that the words in the Scriptures themselves do not contain life but are intended to lead us to the Living Word —Jesus Himself—the only One Who can give "life." We have a pathway to intimacy with Him through Holy Spirit inspired meditation on His Word.

Jeanne Guyon, in her classic book *Experiencing the Depths of Jesus Christ*, teaches a method for "beholding the Lord" through Scripture. After reading a short passage of Scripture, she suggests pausing in gentle quietness and setting your mind on the Spirit and inwardly on Christ:

> "The Lord is found only within your spirit, in the recesses of your being, in the Holy of Holies; this is where He dwells. The Lord once promised to come and make His home within you (John 14:23). He promised to there meet those who worship Him and who do His will. The Lord will meet with you in your spirit. It was St. Augustine who once said that he had lost much time in the beginning of his Christian experience by trying to find the Lord outwardly rather than by turning inwardly."[2]

Supernatural Child Birth

When John and I came on staff at Toronto Airport Christian Fellowship, I was nine months pregnant. On May 24, 1995, we attended a conference at Toronto Airport Christian Fellowship, with speakers Jack Deere and Paul Cain. Near the end of the evening, they shared personal prophetic words the Lord was giving them with several people and I was one who received a prophetic word.

It was a greatly encouraging statement about the anointing and destiny on my children and how the Lord would protect them, "like they were in a safety deposit box, so the Lord will protect your children." After hearing that word, I went down under the power of the Spirit and lay near the front of the church continuing to soak in the Lord's Presence.

After a while, I began to feel contractions as I lay soaking in God's presence. When I shared this with a person praying with me, they got on the microphone and said, "John Bootsma, please

[2] Jeanne Guyon, *Experiencing the Depths of Jesus Christ*, (Jacksonville, FL: SeedSowers Publishing, 1975) p.11.

come to the front, your wife is in labor." John came and helped me up and I was soon in the labor and delivery room at North York General Hospital. Hooked up to a belt-like device that measured my contractions, I watched the needles of the monitor move rapidly each time my abdominal muscles tightened.

However, I was completely oblivious to any pain as I continued to bask in the warmth of God's Presence. I was still soaking in God even while I was in labor! Although I felt no pain, I was aware of my muscles laboring to deliver our child. Lost in the Lord, I shook and trembled under the power of His Presence the entire time. The labor room doctor, a man of 25 years experience, later stated, "That was the most unusual birth I have ever seen." It was a supernatural delivery and we were delighted to welcome our daughter, Aquila, into our lives.

I learned to access that same place of the "weightiness of God's Presence" while in labor during the birth of our next three children and experienced a pain-free, supernatural childbirth each time. How is that possible, you might ask. I learned how to get into God's Presence through meditation upon His Word … and you can do the same.

When my contractions started, I would meditate on a Scripture, repeating it over and over, until I felt myself getting lost in the Glory and Presence of God. Some of my favorite Scriptures to meditate on while in labor were:

"And they who know Your Name will put their trust in You; for You, Lord, have not forsaken those who seek You" (Psalm 9:10).

"The Lord will give strength to His people; the Lord will bless His people with peace" (Psalm 29:11).

"Blessed is the man who fears the Lord, who delights greatly in His commandments" (Psalm 112:1,2).

"I love the Lord, because He has heard my voice and my supplications. Because He has inclined His ear to me, therefore I will call upon Him as long as I live" (Psalm 116:1-2).

The written Word is the door through which you can gain entry to the presence of the Living Word Himself—Jesus.

You Can Plan Your Spiritual Growth

Developing a Bible Study Plan is important to your growth in God. My method is to read a passage from the Old Testament and one from the New Testament each day. I also read a chapter from Proverbs that coincides with the day of the month. In this manner, I continuously read all the way through the Bible in both Old and New Testaments. I believe that leaving out reading the Old Testament creates a handicap in understanding the plan of redemption the Father weaved throughout history. Greater wisdom and understanding comes each time I read a passage again. I gain fresh insight from each rereading of a passage as I ask the Holy Spirit to illuminate its truths.

Paul said to Timothy in 2 Timothy 3:15-17:

"… From childhood you have known the Holy Scriptures, which are able to make you wise for salvation through faith which is in Christ Jesus. All Scripture is given by inspiration of God, and is profitable for doctrine, for reproof, for correction, for instruction in righteousness, that the man of God may be complete, thoroughly equipped for every good work."

If we really believe this passage and want to become equipped for our God-given purpose, then we must act upon it and create a Bible Study Plan!

Notice that Timothy knew the Scriptures from childhood. It is important that we make time each day for teaching the Word of God to our children. John and I have made a habit of reading a portion of Scripture at the breakfast and dinner table as we gather as a family. When the children started coming along, we began reading from a Children's Bible that was accurate to the original texts. We then ask questions about the passage to ensure that everyone listened. That practice has given our children a solid foundation of biblical knowledge. In addition, John helps our children memorize Scripture at bedtime.

Our 15 year old daughter Aquila has a love for the Word which leads her to study the Bible hours a day. Her depth of revelation as a result is remarkable. Eleven year old Zoe has Scripture verses glued to her bedroom wall and recently won our family Bible trivia game. Eight year old Glory Anna memorized and recited for our church Christmas dinner the entire passage of Luke 2:1-20 and has many other passages "hidden in her heart." When I was pregnant with our first child, Judah, the Lord specifically admonished me to read Scriptures aloud over my womb. Since a child in the womb can hear at four months, God's Word was going into his ears and spirit even before birth. Amazingly, when Judah began to crawl and later walk, he would seek out the Bibles in our home and literally chew on them. We marveled at how he recognized the Bible from the other books.

As I write this, he is 19-years-old and already a man of the Word who has developed a Bible study plan of his own. Recently, as Judah was leading worship on his guitar in our House of Prayer, I turned the pages of his Bible for him to get to the Scripture we were singing. I was amazed at all the markings and highlighting he has put in his Bible. Likewise, 17-year-old Gabrielle has a deep understanding of the Word and is particularly knowledgeable about the End Times. Once, in the presence of several World Class Christian Leaders, she asked an End-Time question of Mike Bickle that was so insightful most of the other leaders confessed they did not understand the question (let alone the answer), although Mike did.

THE UNFAILING WAY TO GOD'S APPROVAL

The blood of many martyrs was shed so that you and I could possess a Bible in our language. In 1517, seven believers in Coventry, England were burned at the stake simply for teaching their children to memorize the Lord's Prayer. William Tyndale translated the Scriptures into English, and using a printing press, produced copies that were distributed widely, but he paid a high price. He was strangled and burned at the stake.

The book *Jesus Freaks* tells the story of a Chinese underground church that was raided by police. The believers were told that if they spit on a Bible, which had been placed in the center of the room, they would be allowed to leave unharmed. Starting with the pastor, one by one, each person spit on the Bible and exited the room until it was the turn of a 16 year-old girl. She wiped the spittle off the Bible, and repented for those who had denied and dishonored the Word. The police placed a gun to her head and pulled the trigger.

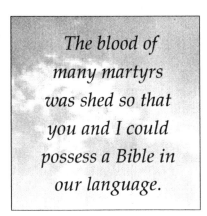

The blood of many martyrs was shed so that you and I could possess a Bible in our language.

We should ask ourselves if we are honoring, studying, and hiding in our hearts, this precious Word that has come to us at so great a cost.

Paul admonishes Timothy in 1 Timothy 4:13 to give attention to the Word and in 2 Timothy 2:15, he emphasizes studying it with the diligence of a worker. "Be diligent to present yourself approved to God, a worker who does not need to be ashamed, rightly dividing the word of truth." The correct application of God's Word requires our diligent study.

Recently, I completed a thorough study of the book of Daniel utilizing commentaries, cross references, and historical facts. What a fascinating book! How exciting to see the prophecies that have already been perfectly fulfilled. That gives us assurance that the end-times prophecies in that book will also come to pass.

If believers took stock of how much time they actually spent in reading and studying the Word of God, most would be shocked at how little time they invest in such an important tool for Christian growth and maturity.

SOAK, SEEK, AND STUDY

These three practices guide the time I spend in "the secret place"

— soaking in God's Presence

— seeking His face through prayer, worship and journaling

— studying His Word

They are simple yet profound keys to finding intimacy with God, hearing His voice, and becoming deeply rooted in Him.

Richard Foster begins his classic book, *Celebration of Discipline: The Path to Spiritual Growth* stating:

"Superficiality is the curse of our age. The doctrine of instant satisfaction is a primary spiritual problem. The desperate need today is not for a greater number of intelligent people, or gifted people, but for deep people."[3]

A deep revelation of the Word of God comes through spending time reading, studying, and meditating on its truths. Pray for God to increase your desire to know His Word and declare that you are gripped with a love for the Scriptures and open to Holy Spirit inspired understanding.

ACTION STEPS

Schedule time each day for meditating on the Word of God.

1. Read a passage from the Old Testament and one from the New Testament each day.

2. Turn each passage into prayer by seeking to connect with the Living Word (Jesus) through the written Word.

3. If a verse admonishes you to obey, then turn it into a declaration such as, "I set my heart to obey you in this directive. Strengthen me to heed your words and build my life on the rock (Matthew 7:24-29) of your commands."

4. Should a passage express a truth to believe, thank God for this truth and ask Him to reveal more of His heart about that truth.

Turn the Word into meditative dialogue with the Author and you will learn to love Him more as you come to know Him better and more intimately through His Word.

[3] Foster, Richard; *Celebration of Discipline*; (New York, NY: HarperCollins Publishers, Inc) 1988.

CHAPTER

8

FACING THE GIANTS IN THE POWER OF THE SPIRIT

"You shall receive power when the Holy Spirit has come upon you"
(Acts 1:8).

CHAPTER 8

Most believers do not realize it, but we are in a war that is fought on many levels. The carnal nature wars against our reborn spirit (Galatians 5). In addition, we wrestle against principalities, rulers of darkness and spiritual hosts of wickedness in the heavenly places (Ephesians 6). These struggles are no surprise to God, His own Son had to defeat evil. When Jesus declared, "It is finished," death was swallowed up in victory.

Applying Jesus' victory to our lives takes us on a journey to wholeness.

Jesus promised the seven churches in Revelation, gifts and rewards for those who overcome the trials of this present age.

Thankfully, we have not been left like orphans to struggle against powers beyond our human capabilities. We are given the same tremendous gift Jesus had to overcome evil and to fulfill His destiny, the Holy Spirit.

Demons in the Bedroom

When I was nineteen years old and living at my parents' house for a summer, I was awakened at 2 am every morning for three weeks with feelings of intense fear. I knew that an evil presence was in my room. I heard voices and saw dark figures. At those times, things would move around in my room, such as a big candle that suddenly fell over; objects on the dresser changed positions, and a poster abruptly fell from the wall. I was petrified!

One dark night, I awoke to find a hooded figure standing beside my bed. I could see him with my natural eyes although I knew he was not a natural being. So frightened that I could barely speak above a whisper, I finally managed to squeak out, "Jesus," and the apparition dissolved like a vapor. I was not involved in witchcraft. "What is going on?" I wondered. I did not understand exactly what these beings were but I knew they were evil.

Two years prior, I had prayed to be filled with the Baptism of the Holy Spirit but nothing seemed to happen. Even though I read in the Book of Acts of the Spirit's power being poured out as a second blessing upon the believers, I had fallen for the lie that this infilling and power was not for me. However, after three weeks of torment, I yearned to be rid of these dark beings, and realized that to be rid of them I needed a power I did not possess. Weary from many sleepless nights, I finally went to a pastor in a nearby city who understood the Holy Spirit and I asked him to pray for me.

I will never forget feeling the fire of the Holy Spirit's power flowing into my being from the top of my head down to my feet. On the drive home, I opened my mouth and the most beautiful language flowed effortlessly from my lips. The Gift of

Tongues, the empowering of the Spirit—it was for me after all! I was so overjoyed, I pulled the car to the side of the road and wept. When I arrived home, I went straight to my bedroom, took authority over those demonic beings tormenting me, and commanded them to leave in Jesus' name. To my utter amazement, it worked and for the first time in three weeks, I slept soundly through the night. I learned from that encounter that the demonic realm was very real and powerful but I also discovered that I was more powerful through the Spirit of God by faith.

That experience changed me for life and the time came when I realized that to be effective I needed to be continuously filled with the Spirit (Ephesians 5:18). Soaking in the Presence of God regularly helps buildup the spirit-man within us. Just as our intellect grows and we gain understanding by studying, our spirit grows based on what we "feed" it and by how much we exercise it through faith-filled actions. Walking in the fulfillment of your personal prophecies requires being empowered by the Holy Spirit.

In addition to the personal prophecies over our lives, there is also the Great Commandment (Matthew 22:37-40), and the Great Commission of Matthew 18-20. We have been given a mission that goes far beyond our human ability, a mandate that demands supernatural empowerment. We cannot accomplish what we have been called to do on our own, and God never intended for us to try. We need the same empowerment Jesus had, the indwelling power of the Holy Spirit.

> *We have been given a mission that goes far beyond our human ability, a mandate that demands supernatural empowerment.*

RANDY CLARK'S SETBACKS AND SUCCESSES

I recently read the autobiography of Randy Clark, the man used of God to spark the revival in Toronto on January 20, 1994. Randy had many failures in his life including his first marriage, a pastorate from which he was forcibly removed, and numerous attempts to heal people with no results. However, Randy did have some powerful prophetic words spoken over his life including a very important one from John Wimber. When John met Randy the first time, the Lord showed John that Randy was going to be powerfully used of God to travel the world as an apostolic leader. At that time, Randy was barely surviving emotionally and financially and could not have been farther from living out that prophetic word.

Later, Randy joined the Vineyard movement, started a church in St. Louis, and travelled to Tulsa and Lakeland to the Rodney Howard-Browne meetings where he received prayer numerous times. Rodney was operating in a powerful ministry of the Holy Spirit and his meetings were characterized by people being "slain in the Spirit," and by "Holy laughter." Randy received an impartation of that anointing which became evident upon his returned to his church and when he ministered at a regional Vineyard meeting. John Arnott heard about the move of the Spirit at the Vineyard meeting and invited Randy to minister at his church in Toronto.

Randy reveals in his book that he was fearful about going to Toronto. He did not know if the Holy Spirit would show up and he did not want to disappoint John and the Toronto church. His fears continued right up to the night before he was to leave home. That evening, a prophetic friend called him (a person who did not know that Randy was going to Toronto) to tell him that the Lord said, "Test me, test me, test me for I will surely back you ..." At that moment, the fear left and Randy knew God would come through and do something in Toronto. He did not realize, however, that a four-day meeting would turn into an outpouring of twelve years of nightly meetings and continue to this day. Randy now travels the globe bringing healing to many and extending the Kingdom of God through the power of the Spirit.

HEIDI BAKER'S BOUNCE BACK FROM BURNOUT

Heidi Baker tells the story of a prophecy she received through Randy Clark while visiting Toronto. It was such a dramatic experience that she was knocked to the floor under the power of the Spirit and remained incapacitated for several days. I remember Heidi being taken in and out of meetings and even to the bathroom in a wheelchair. In the word the Lord spoke to her, He said that He would give Heidi the nation of Mozambique and later give her other nations for the Glory of God. At the time that prophecy was given, the Bakers cared for 300 orphans, had three churches, and owned a few buildings in Maputo, Mozambique. However, they were essentially burned-out and Heidi jokes that she was contemplating getting a job at K-Mart.

One would think that after such a powerful prophetic word and with the amazing signs that followed, the heavens would open on their return to Mozambique but actually, all hell broke loose. The Marxists forcibly took control of their buildings, a large U.S. church poised to give them one million dollars withdrew their donation, a mysterious illness plagued Heidi, and devastating floods hit Mozambique. (Does that make you want to receive a prophetic word?)

Yet, the power of the Spirit had been poured out on Heidi in a way she had never experienced before and she and Rolland refused to give up on their word from God. This may sound trite to you and it is easy to read past it without giving it much thought, however, it is one of those simple, yet profound spiritual truths: IF YOU DO NOT QUIT, YOU WILL WIN!

After the floodwaters receded, the spiritual flood of revival drenched Mozambique. Thousands of people came to hear the gospel and receive a Bible. Churches sprang up overnight and now over 10,000 churches are thriving under the ministry of Rolland and Heidi's ministry called Iris Ministry. They are feeding and educating 7,000 orphans and have centers in many other nations, such as Malawi, South Africa, Sudan, and India. Her prophetic word came to pass through the power of the Holy Spirit, but not in the way they expected.

HE PURPOSES ... WE PROPOSE ... HE PERFECTS

After receiving numerous prophecies regarding missions and ministry as a teenager, I decided that I would become a medical doctor and take my practice onto the mission field in order to fulfill those words. I went to university at age 17 and began taking the required premedical courses, very difficult classes such as Physics, Calculus, Biology, Organic Chemistry, and Physiology. I will never forget that disastrous first semester. For the first time in my life, I failed a test and I was devastated. All my unhealed hurts and insecurities rose up with a fury, but I did complete the year. Then I transferred to the College Nursing program and later returned to the university to complete a Bachelor of Science in Nursing.

I worked in the field of nursing for a few years before giving it up to become a full-time mother and wife. I died to the dream of becoming a missionary. However, God resurrected that dream in His way ... in His time ... through the power of the Spirit. The Lord revealed to me years ago, as I was basking in His Presence, that He could do anything. He was all-powerful, and He would accomplish those things that He purposed for my life. That was a life-changing revelation, not something I merely read in a book or intellectually understood. I believe it for my life and I know it is true for your life, too. God is so powerful and so very faithful.

Word or No Word, You Have a Divine Destiny

People have asked me the question, "What if I don't have prophetic words over my life? How will I know what to do?" The answer is simple. You do have words over your life. The Scriptures make clear the blueprint for our lives. We are to make the Sermon on the Mount our lifestyle. We are to fulfill the Great Commandment to love God and others, and the Great Commission to spread the Good News. We are to know salvation, live in His love and extend it to others, and walk in victory.

What excites you? What burns in your heart? What do you enjoy doing? Step into the things you like to do and God will correct your course as needed.

A friend of mine, who is not called to a platform ministry,

> *What excites you? What burns in your heart? What do you enjoy doing? Step into the things you like to do and God will correct your course as needed.*

recently discovered she is good at organizing Christian movie nights at our church and is talented at producing funny video announcements. She is enhancing the body of Christ by simply doing that which she does well and enjoys.

Walking In Obedience to Your Word

After being Associate Pastors in Toronto for eight years, my husband and I were asked to move from Toronto to Stratford to be Senior Pastors of the Stratford church that John and Carol Arnott had originally founded. A great honor perhaps but it felt like a depressing assignment to me. The party was in Toronto and leaving the Well of Revival to resurrect a church in a sleepy little city did not appeal to me. However, the Lord seemed to think it was a good idea and He gave us dreams and words that made it clear that it was His will for us to make this move.

Quite literally, I cried everyday for the first six months after moving to Stratford. I experienced the sensation of having a tight band wrapped around my head that felt like demonic oppression. The city streets were founded on the free masonry symbol. A large Shakespearian Theatre Festival attracted seasonal visitors but was not known for its godliness. Drugs were reported to be a problem, particularly in the high schools. The church had decreased in size since John and Carol left to found the Toronto church and it was lacking in the Presence of God and fruitfulness.

When we moved into our brand new home, a plumbing problem brought sewage into our newly carpeted basement area. On moving day, my son had a hot dog get stuck in his throat and we had to rush him to the local hospital and then on to a larger city hospital to have it removed. What a battle!

In the midst of this the Lord spoke, "I do not send you out to war to lose. I send you to win!" In praying for His strategy for victory, the Lord clearly said, "I want you to worship and I want you to pray." He went on to say, "The River and the Tabernacle of David are going to meet and form a spontaneous combustion." I remember thinking, "What does that mean and exactly what is the Tabernacle of David?" I began a study of the Scriptures and made several trips to the International House of Prayer in Kansas City, to study their 24/7 House of Prayer. It operated in the spirit of the Tabernacle of David which Amos 9:11 and Acts 15 prophesy will be rebuilt in the last days.

John and I gave our mornings to the Lord in prayer, worship, and seeking His face. Later, we took this daily commitment to the church building where others joined us. For six years now, we have led a House of Prayer. Presently, it operates for 15 hours weekly in anointed Harp and Bowl worship and Intercession (Revelation 5) and the change has been dramatic. As the Presence of God began to sweep through our church, prodigal sons and daughters came home to salvation, healings and miracles began to occur regularly. Growth sprung forth both numerically and in the hearts of believers. Drug houses in the city began to be discovered and shutdown by police and one spontaneously burned down.

The mayor of our city contacted my husband about starting a Mayor's Prayer Breakfast. It has now become an annual event with 300 of the city's business, political, and church leaders in attendance to hear the truth of the gospel proclaimed and to pray corporately. The flier for the last prayer breakfast had a picture of our city hall and the verse under it read, "My house shall be called a house of prayer." On another side of the page were the words, "Jesus Christ is Lord." What incredible statements for a city to make!

Reports have come from other life-giving churches of Stratford citing growth and transformation. Indeed the Lord sent us into a war zone, but it was not to lose, it was to proclaim victory and advance the Kingdom through the power of prayer and worship. He clearly said in Isaiah 56:7, which was quoted by Jesus in the gospels: "My house shall be called a house of prayer."

I believe it is the Father's heart for every city and every nation to walk in sustained, corporate prayer and worship, and see the transformation of hearts, families, businesses, and their communities.

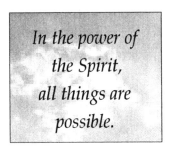

In the power of the Spirit, all things are possible.

Indeed "the knowledge of the glory of the Lord will fill the earth" (Habakkuk 2:14). The Lord is looking for those who will not hide from the battle and merely wait to be "whisked away." He is seeking those who will step onto the frontlines to conquer and occupy this world until Jesus returns to establish His full rule and reign. "The weapons of our warfare are not carnal but mighty in God for pulling down strongholds" (2 Corinthians 10:4). Therefore, let us use our weapons of prayer, worship, and declarations of the Word of God in the power of the Spirit.

To Fulfill Our Mission, We Need To ...

Spend time each day being refilled with the Spirit for we must abide in His strength to walk in the fullness of victory. In the power of the Spirit, all things are possible.

CONCLUDING COMMENTS FOR WALKING
IN YOUR PROMISES

Walking in the fullness of destiny and prophecy is conditional upon our response.

What God has said in His Word is true. What He has said over your life is true. He is a God of fulfilled prophecy.

If we are willing to pay the price, we will walk in fulfillment of every promise given us and every word spoken over us. Ezekiel 12:23, 25, 28:

> "The days are at hand, and the fulfillment of every vision ... For I am the Lord, I speak, and the word which I speak will come to pass; it will no more be postponed; for in your days ... I will say the word and perform it," says the Lord God ... Therefore say to them, "Thus says the Lord God: 'None of My words will be postponed any more, but the word which I speak, will be done,' says the Lord God."

1. God is looking for men and women who know who they are, discern what they are called to do, and are determined to walk in their destiny, to play their part in heaven's invasion of earth.

2. Truly knowing the One who has loved and called us is essential to our success. In fact, the Great Commandment is to love Him, and loving Him means we must come to realize that He loves us personally. We become what we behold. The revelation of the Father's love for us has no end. Understanding God's love sets the stage for us to receive healing from life's

wounds and for our hearts to spring forth with life (Proverbs 4:23). We become disentangled from our web of hurts, offenses, unforgiveness, and bitterness when we allow God's goodness to embrace us.

3. As we seek a place of intimacy with Him, our spirit is opened to revelation. As His sheep, we are to know the voice of the Good Shepherd so He can lead us into the place of fullness. He awakens prophetic gifting in us and allows us to receive revelation in order to transform and prepare us to reform the world around us.

Grounding and meditation in the written Word enables us to connect with the Living Word—Jesus. Declaration of His Word, as well as His promises over our lives takes us into fruitful abundance because life and death are in the power of the tongue (Proverbs 18:21).

My prayer for you, the reader, is for the anointing to be poured out upon you for your journey from the land of promises and prophecies into the Promised Land of fulfillment and destiny. This joyous pilgrimage is ours to take through the fullness of the Spirit that dwells within us. Enjoy the journey!